BRUSH CAT

Also by Jack McEnany

Bode: Go Fast, Be Good, Have Fun

BRUSH CAT

ON TREES,
THE WOOD ECONOMY,
AND THE MOST DANGEROUS
JOB IN AMERICA

JACK McENANY

ST. MARTIN'S PRESS ⚞ NEW YORK

BRUSH CAT. Copyright © 2009 by Jack McEnany. All rights reserved.
Printed in the United States of America. For information,
address St. Martin's Press, 175 Fifth Avenue, New York, N.Y. 10010.

www.stmartins.com

Designed by William Ruoto

Library of Congress Cataloging-in-Publication Data

McEnany, Jack.
Brush cat : on trees, the wood economy, and the most dangerous job in
America / Jack McEnany.—1st ed.
p. cm.
ISBN-13: 978-0-312-36891-3
ISBN-10: 0-312-36891-7
1. Lumber trade—New England. 2. Logging—New England.
3. Loggers—New England. I. Title.
HD9757.N3M34 2009
331.7'634980974—dc22

2008035450

First Edition: March 2009

10 9 8 7 6 5 4 3 2 1

For Becky, Fiona, and Liam,
who, poor things,
have to live with me

CONTENTS

ACKNOWLEDGMENTS

The cast herein has my eternal respect and gratitude for all that they did for me, and all that they are the rest of the time. Many, many thanks to Bob Benson, who cut down my trees and planted the seed; my agent, Susan Raihofer, of the David Black Agency; Phil Revzin, of St. Martin's Press, a kind and patient editor; Jen Crawford, always one step ahead; Rusty Dewees, Bob Santy, Rick Santy, and Steve Santy, Ray Murphy, Judy and Jay Hoeschler, Tim Emperor, John Harrigan, Gerard Lavoie, Jim Mathews, Sarah Smith, Mike Guyer, Tom Wagner, John Aber, Cathy Corkery, Jasen Stock, David Pickman, Donnie at Exit 41, Timber Tina, Steve Hamburg, Dave, Jim, and Mike, Ron Wyman, Peter and Christi Gignac, Nip, Roland Shick, Spencer Larabee, Eric Kingsley, Phil Bryce, Laurie Wayburn, Jack Savage, Paul Doscher, Kathryn Conant, Jim Wagner, Fred Moody, Jim Becht, Pat Herlihy, Joe Bergeron, Tom Workman, and Mauricio.

BRUSH CAT

Damp, humid green all over the place—gives the country an unhealthy look. I guess I really am a desert rat. The sound of all these verdant leafy things breathing and sweating and photosynthesizing around me all the time makes me nervous. Trees, I believe (in the ardor of my prejudice), like men, should be well spaced off from one another, not more than one to a square mile. Space and scarcity give us dignity. And liberty. And thereby beauty.

Edward Abbey

INTRODUCTION

I live in the heart of the Great Northern Forest, at the high tip of Franconia Notch, New Hampshire. All across the United States, only the state of Maine has a larger percentage of its territory covered in forest. To us, the woods are as ever-present and essential as the ocean is to the people living on a small island.

I first moved here on a lark in the spring of 1984. I passed through Franconia Notch, which serves as a break against the weather and civilization, and never looked back. I rented a cabin—two and a half rooms of uninsulated moldiness on the bank of the Ham Branch River, the nicest feature of which was a woodstove with glass doors on the front. I bought a bundle of camp wood outside the supermarket, and after I scraped the soot from the glazing on the stove's doors with a razor blade, I could see the flames inside and found it comforting, like the television fireplace at Christmas. This was many years ago; I've since learned that a welded, heavy steel gauge, airtight box with an outside air intake is the perfect woodstove. Wood is too precious, expensive, and heavy to waste on Bing Crosby–style coziness.

I ordered the six cords that the wood guy, whose number I found on the cabin's refrigerator, told me I'd need to adequately (as opposed to comfortably) heat the place. It sounded like a lot, but I didn't want to get caught short. On the other hand, this was a rental and I didn't want a lot of wood that I'd have to move or forfeit when I took up residence someplace less moldy.

The wood arrived a few weeks later—dumped in my tiny driveway while I was out. A single cord is eight feet by eight feet by four feet, stacked. This I learned by calling the County Extension Service. So, six cords of firewood in a single pile looks like the rubble of a bombed-out building. As far as I could see, just stacking that much wood was easily a year's worth of heavy lifting. I'd never heated with wood before, never even lived anywhere with a working fireplace. But if the cavemen managed it, I was reasonably sure I could, too. But I've been wrong before.

Spring in the North Country is chilly, so I brought a couple of pieces of green wood into the house to fire up the stove. I didn't know that unseasoned wood throws no heat and clogs your chimney with creosote, an oily, flammable by-product of bad planning. But it wasn't an issue because I couldn't get the sticks into the stove. I monkeyed with it awhile, assuming I had the wrong angle or was doing something so obviously ass-backward that I'd feel stupid about it later. But the problem with this wood delivery was that the logs were a couple of inches too long to fit in the stove. Even after I figured out the problem,

I still felt stupid. I knew then that heating with wood was more difficult than I'd imagined. Just like everything else.

I was a bit ruffled when I realized that the wood was simply too long. I owned a large pile of eighteen-inch sticks when I needed sixteen, tops. It was my fault, but the wood guy had delivered to my cabin before. When I'd first called him, he'd said, "I know the place." But when I called him back to say the wood was too long, his response was, "Yeah? I don't know what you got for a stove in there. You call me for wood, I give you what you ask for. Eighteen-inch is pretty standard. You need something else, you need to say so. Most people know what they need."

Implying that I didn't, which was a fair point. I may have been a flatlander and an idiot when it came to ordering firewood, but I was smart enough to know that he wouldn't be stopping by anytime soon with a corrected wood order and a 10-percent-off card for my trouble. I had told him eighteen-inch sticks, because that's what it said on the note. So either the note was a cruel joke or this was a different stove. But it didn't matter. This was my first encounter with a logger; my subsequent decades-long dealings with them have only slightly improved.

In order to clip off the last two inches (I later learned that it made more sense to simply cut the logs in half), I bought my first chainsaw. I was lucky in a way; it was Memorial Day so I rose extra early and went for a cruise up north in my new/old canary-yellow Jeep Comanche. Yard sales abound on this holiday, people selling things on the side of the road, or up side streets located by following sketchy maps stapled to telephone poles. A lot of it is the same junk the seller bought from someone else last year.

I needed everything from dishes to bookcases, to tables and chairs, to . . . everything. I didn't even have a proper can opener; I was using one of those cheap little camping keys that assumes your major entertainment for the night is tending a fire while trying to open a can of beans. So I set out to fundamentally outfit myself that day and did so for under a hundred dollars. Including the purchase of chainsaw.

Early in the day, my first stop, I found it—a Husquie, which I'd heard good things about. Bright orange and interesting to look at with its switches and geegaws, like the big-boy toy that it was, all cleaned up nice and shiny, too. I hefted it with both hands as if I were testing the weight and balance of a broadsword; I moved it through the air in front of me, imagining the sound of it in my head, smelling the blue-brown two-stroke exhaust. I pictured myself heroically felling giant pine trees and ripping through that pile of slightly oversized firewood like a light saber through chocolate bars.

"It was my bastardly ex-husband's," the woman in charge said, a smoldering Virginia Slims hanging off her lower lip. "What do you give me?" I had no idea what a used chainsaw was worth, or just how used this one was. But I had overheard her say that she was moving to Florida. "I don't think he ever cut anything with it all," she said. "Not that I saw, anyway. Complained about his back all the time."

I toyed with the choke, yanked the cord three times, and it fired right up—vibrating, whining, clearly wanting to cut loose and rip into something. It was a tool with an obvious purpose. I quickly shut it off, because, frankly, the damn thing scared me. And that just made me want it all the more. Presuming no sentimental attachment, I offered her fifty dollars and she smiled with her hand out. For another five bucks it came with a "barely opened" gallon of bar oil and a bunch of "barely used" round files. A round file is about the size and shape of a number 1 pencil, and you lightly twist it as you run it along the chain's dulled and chipped teeth, and then flatten out the rakers. Doing both perfectly as often as necessary is the difference between a saw that cuts and a saw that doesn't. It took me ten years to figure that out.

I traded that saw and have borrowed and owned more since. I didn't like any of them. I've also followed too many loggers into too many woodlots, and probably too many barrooms, annoying them with questions about the simplest things: What's stumpage? What's doomage? Is logging safe? Bunchers, skidders, harvesters, forwarders—what's the difference? Cutting lumber, selling cordwood, chipping pecker poles for wood chips . . . what's the best gig?

More than one Brush Cat told me to "get the book." But there is no book; it's logger-speak for "learn the trade." Or maybe in my case it meant learn something, *anything*. I've been writing *Brush Cat* in my head for more than twenty years and now I've put it on paper. It's about loggers and their machines, and the most dangerous job in America, but it's also about the essentialness of wood, in all its hide-in-plain-sight ubiquity.

Not only do most Americans live in houses made of wood filled with wooden furniture, they also want to press Print on their computer whenever they like, use the bathroom with impunity, and never worry about where the paper comes from, or why it's so cheap. They want endless newspapers, magazines, lottery tickets, tampons, Venti to-go cups at Starbucks—it's a wood-intensive world we live in. In fact, we are a culture of wood and unlikely ever to change. We'll be reading big fat books at the beach and cleaning up with paper towels long after the oil economy is a museum-quality memory and chainsaws run on hydrogen cells.

This book is all about trees, but it's mainly about people. Loggers, lumberjacks, waitresses, mill owners, murderers, birlers, log rollers, chainsaw carvers, hikers, lobbyists, surveyors, chainsaw dealers, Logger Bob, poets, bureaucrats, charlatans, Sugar Hill Ladies, politicians, Timber Tina, businessmen, actors. All play roles big and small in the culture of the forest all too often overlooked by those of us who see only trees.

It's also, inevitably, about politics, actually geopolitics. Well-managed working forests are a major piece in turning back the damage of climate change, through the generation of electricity using wood chips, and the sequestration of CO_2 in standing forestlands. The price of wood and wood chips, closely tied to the price of the energy and labor needed to produce them, exerts a huge micropull on supply and demand.

And it's above all about the future. New Hampshire is a prime case study for the future of logging. It's the second-most-forested state in the nation, with a four-hundred-year history of using the woods to survive. We continue to rely heavily on our forestland, but the future is at best uncertain. Modernity in the form of rising fuel costs and diminishing oil reserves, prohibitive insurance rates, expensive medical care, onerous state and federal regulations, environmentalism, corporatism, and globalization negatively impact the logging industry every day. The logger is the unseen procurer who attends to the small matter of harvesting three-ton giants and transporting them down a mountainside, out of the woods, unscarred, and to the mill. You'd think such efficient and specialized operational skills would carry a fair return in the free market. But you'd be wrong.

Every wood-based product we use—and there are ten thousand and counting—started with some guy trudging into the woods with a chainsaw. This book is about that guy, his job, and how it affects us all.

1

THE BRUSH CAT
OF THE
GREAT NORTHERN FOREST

*Country in which there are precipitous
cliffs with torrents running between,
deep natural hollows, confined places,
tangled thickets, quagmires and
crevasses, should be left with all possible
speed and not approached.*
  Sun Tzu

 The green strip of land along the northern
edge of most maps of the United States is dense green
forest, like a horizontal Chile with no beachfront, or
a soft-serve Arctic National Park. The eastern corner is the Great
Northern Forest—twenty-six million acres of dense woodlands

that spread from Maine's Mount Katahdin through New Hampshire's White Mountains, over to Vermont's Green Mountains, up into New York's Adirondacks, and finally ending in the Tug Hill region of upstate New York, close to Canada.

There are lakes and fields, rivers and swamps throughout the Great Northern Forest, but mostly it's a jungle of thickets and canopies, pine groves, and hardwoods, the dead ones sprawled on the living, their towering mass clouding everything near and above. It's natural to feel small or lost in such a battered old cathedral, especially at midday, when you can lose sight of the sky. All around you on the ground, downer trees lie like giant Pick Up Sticks, each resting precariously on the one that fell before it, creating a nearly impenetrable coppice.

A Brush Cat is a logger who works woods like these the way a farmer plows his fields. His job is to see beyond the natural state and its wanton carnage—the blow-downs and ice-storm detritus, whole stands of ant-infested hulks still standing, pretending to be alive—and pluck the keepers from the wilding crop. If he's good at it, it's like picking flowers in a meadow, except heavier and with a lot more noise and mud.

It's a surreal scene this far off the well-trodden trail, seeing up close the off-the-trail stuff forbidden to hikers—spots so green and wet and humanly impassable that even the moose go around. In this part of the Great Northern Forest, sharp, mossy granite outcroppings are common. They're lichen-covered monsters, like variegated tall ships jutting up through the earth's crust, anchored in the deep woods with birch trees muckled onto them like giant squids growing off their sides at impossible angles, gripping them with roots like tentacles, their trunks twisted heliotropically up through the canopy, toward the sun.

During the last ice age, glaciers scraped along, plowing up the earth and making mountains. They dragged outcroppings as big as dirigibles for thousands of miles until they finally broke off or rolled away. Other granite leavings are in evidence, too, some small and grabby enough to trap your ankle forever in a tiny, hidden valley from which no sound ever escapes.

The logger cuts his way into these woods on a narrow road called a skid row, and it's not a coincidence that Skid Row denotes a seedy neighborhood in any American city. Historically and etymologically, skid rows gained that reputation because, a long time ago, they were the parts of town favored by loggers on leave from the camp. The Brush Cats, by most accounts, were a load of reprobates, and, deserved or not, that's a tough reputation to shake.

But to actually cut a skid row into the woods as long and wide as it needs to be, and no more, the logger maneuvers in and around boulders, over cliffs, up steep embankments, always plotting, strategizing his way in and out. Nothing here in the deep dark woods is straightforward or predictable. The single fact that a logger can count on is that no matter how much it looks like it might, a tree will never fall uphill. And that's it. Nevertheless, the vast majority of logging deaths are caused by people dropping trees on their own heads, or someone else's.

And that's nearly what we were doing, Bob Benson and I. Or at least I thought so. It was our first week in the woods together, and we were laying down a skid row in order to harvest the lot. Or he was, anyway. I was probably just in the way. It was January in northern New Hampshire and we'd been seven hours out in the wind and cold, locked halfway into the annual six-week-long aeon of thirty-below-zero weather. Climactic conditions were openly hostile to human life—the cold could freeze exposed skin in less than thirty minutes. It hurt just to breathe—the smallest inhalation instantly crystallizing into a throbbing ice-cream headache.

Behind me, Bob's squalling, tricked-out chainsaw abruptly choked off and I heard that solitary and unmistakable *crack*, its echo bouncing off Mount Kinsman, all the way over on the other side of the valley. Bob had cut a giant maple somewhere in the woods not far behind me, and as it collapsed, its wide-reaching canopy swept through the trees above us. Like the T. rex in *Jurassic Park*, I felt the danger long before it arrived. The toppling began as a light rumble, as if a flock of birds was taking wing, but quickly grew into a gushing-whooshing-chasing haunt, coming up faster behind me as I skedaddled into the bush beneath the pine boughs, my chainsaw stalled in my right hand, my eyes and legs going dodgy in opposite directions, seeking out any cover.

When the woods were quiet and still again, I wiped the snow off the lenses of my safety glasses and saw that the tree had dropped to my left, and perhaps wasn't on a collision course with the top of my head after all. Logger Bob knew what he was doing. He's a pro; I'm a neophyte, and any mistakes made were entirely my fault.

Bob came bounding out of the brush, a big grin on his face. "You see her come down? Slicker than shit, huh, really nice!" he said. He pronounced "nice" *noice*.

"Beauty," I said.

"Fuckin'-A *roight* it was a beauty," Bob replied. "Perfect landing." He smiled at me again, and Bob's got a big smile by anyone's standards. His ungloved hand gripped the trunk as if he were taking its pulse. "Got to be done right," he said. "This old girl's been in the world a long time."

Nobody bothers to yell "Timber!" anymore. Loggers wear hearing protection, or risk getting fined by the labor inspector if he rolls onto the job site—so yelling is pointless. And that's if they ever did yell "Timber!" because Bob told me he's never heard it anywhere but in Looney Tunes.

The problem is that Bob is accustomed to working alone, and forgets I'm with him sometimes. When he's most aware of my presence, it's because he wants to show somebody something interesting, such as the dense and ancient dendrochronology on a big fat stump, or a gouge in the lithosphere that exposes the china-brittle shale stone that the mountain under our feet sat on.

Mostly, however, he's focused on the task at hand, like an artist or an athlete performing at his highest level. And that's why I nearly ended up pounded into the forest floor like a tent stake. His kind of logging isn't a team sport. Brush Cats are careful, and as a point of pride look out for one another, but they all know that the best set of eyes looking out for you is your own. When Bob remembers I'm around, he keeps me behind him with the same hand signals he uses on his dog. I'm usually more obedient than Kodi, but not today. Kodi's a big Siberian husky with big blue eyes. He's not a puppy anymore, but he still pants that same endlessly reckless energy, and bolts for the woods, like the wolf that people mistake him for, at every opportunity.

Bob is up for it. He sees a lot of himself in that dog. He's lean and muscular, late forties, with a quick smile and an unmistakable basso voice. He skis religiously, bikes interminably, and studies yoga. If fifty is the new thirty, Bob is the proof.

I defer to Bob out here in the Great Northern Forest the way I would to the ship's captain if we were fishing the North Atlantic. He's a highly skilled technician who can not only run all the gear, and fix it, too, but can identify trees by the texture of their bark and the smell of their leaves. He says he can see rot in the heartwood before it's cut, and can drop a tree as tall as an apartment building within an inch of where he said it would fall. He's outwardly unaffected by sawdust in his eyes, and doesn't care about the heat, the cold, or swarming, biting bugs. Not even bad business deals keep Bob down; he just keeps coming, sanguine in every way. They all do.

I was on the job to cut and split firewood, because Bob's regular firewood guy—we'll call him Mark—was up at the Coos County Farm doing an eight-month bit for being a "habitual offender." I knew a few things about Mark—mostly that his relationship with law enforcement was not good because he suffers from an insatiable thirst for beer. I've also heard that he has more ex-wives than fingers, but that might be an exaggeration. Bob doesn't care about any of that because with a chainsaw in his stubby mitts, Mark is one hellacious Brush Cat who works like a small army and complains only when the money is slow.

According to Logger Bob, Mark hadn't had a license in eight years because of what he thought was a seventeen-hundred-dollar fine hanging over his head from his penultimate pinch, which was his second conviction for DUI. Turned out that it was only a seventy-dollar fine that he owed, but he'd never hired a lawyer, and so he didn't get that good news until his third arrest for impaired driving.

"Stupid all around," said Bob. "If being habitually offensive will get you busted, the jails around here are going to fill up pretty damn quick."

Mark's incarceration meant that Bob lost an integral part of his operation in a hardwood lot such as this. But what frustrated him most was that the county put its prisoners out in the woods logging—using what Bob called "slave labor" to compete directly against guys like him. "Talk about the double whammy," he said. "Not only is Mark gone, but he's gone over to the enemy."

It's for this reason, and this reason alone, that Bob agreed to have a yutz like me with him in the woods, "for as long as we can stand each other." He had little choice. He needed what modicum of help I could offer. And I work cheap, which is to say free, and that's certainly a factor. I did virtually no logging; I did what any fool would do in the presence of a master at work—I watched. And also about what I'm worth. This arrangement is actually a step up in our business relationship: a few years ago I had Bob do some logging on my property. When I pulled out my saw and put on my Kevlar chaps to work with him, he said that if I was going to help, he'd have to charge me double.

But here we were, finally, working in the woods together, standing over this wooden hulk. Even lying on its side, it was three stories high. When a big tree is felled, it's divided up into three parts. First is the slash, the useless brush, which is usually left behind. Studies show that it impedes forest regeneration and increases the risk and intensity of forest fires. Loggers say it replenishes the soil that the trees left behind are growing in. And they're both right.

This was a maple, a hardwood, so its limbs would be cut and split for firewood, the denuded trunk then dragged to the landing, sliced into prescribed lengths, trucked to the mill, and shaved down to veneer for furniture and cabinets. If it had been white pine, it would have been cut up into lumber for the construction industry. The quicker all this unfolds, the more profitable Bob's month is. And that also depends on the value of the wood on the lot. That maple makes the week worthwhile, but other trees that grow in weedy abundance—perfectly good trees for lumber—don't bring the same dollar. Tamarack, also known as the American larch, for instance, is not a sought-after wood, but, as construction material goes, one logger told me, "When it dries, it's as hard as Chinese arithmetic." I happen to think all arithmetic is hard, but I take his point.

But none of this postfelling cleanup had happened yet. We were still in the moment of the kill, and the tree lay there still and huge, like a belly-up dragon slain when he wasn't looking. When you get up that close to a horizontal tree, you see that a fully grown maple is quite a substantial thing—if you could get your arms around it, it would take a hundred more just like you to muscle it out of the woods, a single step at a time. There are enough board feet of lumber in it to build a cabin, with enough left over to heat it for a winter.

This was a big tree, four or five tons, more than seventy feet tall. Bob climbed all over it, limbing it down to the trunk, then drawing out his tape measure to notch it for lengths. Some of the branches he carved off were as big around and long as a freestanding tree. He jumped over gnarly limbs, balancing on one as he zipped the next as meticulously as picking lint from a sweater. When he was done, the trunk was long and lean, like a ragged telephone pole.

Bob used his saw with the authority of a Benihana chef and the careful mien of a man who'd been laid low by a bad move somewhere along the line. He's actually lucky that his knee bothers him only when it's wet, because he can't work then anyway. It's ACL damage, chunks of cartilage all bound up in the works. But his knees hurt mostly from skiing, not logging. Bob has survived twenty-five years in the woods by being a safe logger. That's the only way to do it. But even hyper-vigilance is no guarantee of survival.

If chainsaws were coffeemakers, then mine would be a single-cup drip and Bob's would be a giant samovar, or one of those Cadillac espresso machines at Starbucks. Meaning that his is a real logger's saw, the industrial grade, not some dainty electric job meant for trimming the Japanese maple in the garden, or a consumer model available at your big-box store, designed to look like the real deal but with a chain that, for safety's sake, can't cut beans. Like mine. A genuine lumberman's rig is your father's chainsaw on juice—a 120-decimal, rabid, vibrating wolverine that any sane man holds as far from his person as he can. Loggers, in my mind, are like snake handlers, or lion tamers—dauntless, scrappy, and afraid of nothing but a mad mother bear.

A saw kicks when the tip catches the wood at an oblique

angle, which is rarely a hazard to someone who knows what he's doing, but we all make mistakes. It's an occupational hazard, and only one of the many. Logging is by far the most dangerous job in America, and not all from chainsaws. The last injury Bob suffered was from a log rolling off the top of a pile and hitting his right leg, bending it in ways it shouldn't. Locally, those aren't the injuries people remember. Where people work in the woods, chainsaw misadventures are like Prussian dueling scars, and everybody's got one.

Unfortunately, all the OSHA rules and certification classes in the world can't mitigate the inherent dangers in logging. It's perilous work. According to the U.S. Department of Labor, it's the most dangerous job in America, with 118 deaths per one hundred thousand workers, handily beating out the number-two killer profession, commercial fishing, at 71 deaths per one hundred thousand. Pilots and navigators come in at number three with 70 deaths per, and iron workers fourth with 58 deaths.

So, on a perfect summer day, with a clear blue sky, logging is still more dangerous than anything else you can do to draw a paycheck, including high-wire circus performer, SWAT commando, and swordswallower. Add to the risk the fact that January in the Northeast is inhumanly cold. If you're injured in the woods, immobilized in any way—ravaged by a rabid fox, pinned by a fallen tree, or cut deeply and viscerally—there's every chance that you'll freeze to death before anything else kills you.

It's so cold at this time of year that snow is as dry as dust. Normally it's 75 percent or more water, but when temperatures drop into negative numbers for an extended period, the ice in a lake, a river, or even in the frozen ground below is warmer than the air above. Ice actually sublimates moisture from the snow, wringing the water from it, and leaving the flakes so crispy that they squeal underfoot like crumpled Styrofoam. The advantage is that the logs slide easily on it, and, as always, Brush Cats take the good with the bad.

The long periods of life-threatening cold might encourage some to take a vacation. And they do, when there's time and money. Every logger has a piece of property on his to-do list that sits on the other side of a wetland, accessible only in the deepest freeze, so that's when they do it. The colder, the better. There are five advantages to working at this time of year, as enumerated by Bob:

- *No bugs.*
- *With all the leaves off the deciduous trees, it's easier to see what, if anything, is worth bushwhacking.*
- *The days are short, and you can't cut trees at night (at least you're not supposed to).*
- *In case of an accident, blood flows significantly slower.*
- *No bugs.*

This particular woodlot—the earth is divided between water, woodlots, and the rest of the world—was a disaster. After years of what purists would call the natural state and loggers would call neglect, we were there to fix it without doing any further harm. Most of it was commercially useless because of the

ice storm of 1997, which felled millions of board feet of softwood and left layers of busted and snapped trees on the ground.
It was a Paul Bunyanesque bonfire waiting for a spark. Bob
offered it up as a prime example of the unmanaged forest. For
him, the forest is the monster lurking over the garden wall that
must be faced, and conquered. He's a conservationist and an
outdoorsman; but a woodlot is a field to be prudently harvested,
while the wilderness is something else altogether. And Bob
knows the difference,

An untended and overgrown forest is chaos, an impossible-
to-penetrate jungle, and incomprehensible if you get turned
around inside it. Without a compass, it's the easiest place on
earth to get lost. There are thousands of natural markers, and
they all look exactly alike. Trees in this forest are like shampoo
at the supermarket—more varieties than you can count. It's a
thicket of towering woody weeds, the living, growing evidence
of a rampant and indiscreet ecesis—the elms, and gnarly maples,
the pin cherries, a copse of high-grade hardwoods, birch, red
maples, black cherries. This is a boreal forest, named for Boreas,
the Greek god of the north wind. So there's a slew of conifers
with their waxy needles and antifreeze sap that makes them
hardier and better-suited than their broad-leafed cospecies. In a
spruce-moose forest, there are moose who, like the spruce, prefer
it wet, and then there's the spruce, of course, and the cedar, fir,
juniper, hemlock, balsam, tamarack, and lots of white pine. The
whole forest grows in and around itself, every species competing
for space, light, and moisture. And when they finally succeed,
when they reach for the light and make it their own, down they
come.

A smart logger, one with an eye to the future, looks to glean the good wood and cull the bad. He also wants to manage the harvest in such a way that the immature money trees aren't barked or snapped or just plain run over. The woods are a renewable resource only if you leave behind a healthy crop. Like everyone else, he has obligations to meet, and wants to handle business as few times as possible. It's also nice to make a few bucks at the end of the month. That, after all, is the point.

Winter in the forest is so quiet even the small noises seem to echo. The big trees—the widow-makers—crackle and snap when the wind sways them just the slightest. But there are no birds, no squirrels or chipmunks. The inhabitants of the woods are either dead, asleep, or moving very slowly. Other than moose and deer, rodents and raptors, coyotes, ermines, sparrows, fishers, and the odd, errant bobcat, there's not much happening. When it's this cold, for this long, hunting becomes secondary to staying warm, leaving little traffic in the woods.

But even when they are out and about, both predators and prey are deathly quiet—until they meet up. When a coyote snares a snowshoe hare, or a fisher's on a barn cat, the logger—who's already alone in the dark and cold forest—often hears the introduction clearly, and it always sounds like somebody strangling a baby. From my mercifully limited experience, that pained and twisted squeal off in the woods feels like the bathwater going cold around me. Other than that—and the clatter of chainsaws and heavy equipment, of course—the woods are a nice quiet place in winter.

At a granular level, under these conditions, the physical world decelerates into molasses mode. Thirty-weight motor oil gets as thick as tar; diesel fuel gels up like hair mousse. Nothing mechanical operates properly, if it runs at all. It's metal-on-metal out there—a hard, unlubricated grind that scores the valves and pistons, shortening the motor's life, as it does everyone's. Still, in the logging trade, the weather is never the worst of it. No matter how raw, cold, hot, wet, or snowy, there's plenty to keep a logger's mind off the weather.

Late in the day we waited down at the landing for the logging truck to arrive. Bob sharpened his saw on the tailgate of his truck, while Kodi gnawed a three-foot length of birch, and I ate an energy bar.

"You always have to keep your saw sharp," he said, not for nothing. "A dull saw is more dangerous than a sharp one."

"Like when Dale Earnhardt said slower is faster?" I asked. Because I don't know what the hell that meant, either.

I finished my energy bar, got my saw out of the back of the truck, and went to work at it with my round file. Bob looked closely at my angle of attack, let me sharpen a few teeth, and then said, "Not like that." He reached for the saw and smiled. "We need all your appendages attached." It's attention to detail that's kept Bob healthy and in business all these years. One small distraction can end a logger's career, or life.

Finally, mercifully, the end of the day came, at four thirty in the afternoon, and it was already dark. The light on the snow quickly faded from dappled to subfusc, and the Presidential Range of the White Mountains stood in the darkening distance, an immovable barrier that separates us from the flats, the big cities and their sprawl, from all the good jobs and most of the bad crimes. We drove past colorless swayback houses, sometimes one with a collapsing barn leaning into it, the mechanic, with his bay door open and a green bottle of beer to his lips, waving as we passed, his yellow-eyed, chained-up mutt peering from the doghouse at us. We passed the used-baby-clothes store, the pizza place, the old folks' home, the church, the big square and featureless town hall, and the tiny police station with its one small blue light out front.

By the time I trudged into the bar, the sky had begun to fill with stars. "Beer thirty" often bookends the day for those who bump into one another at breakfast. These days, Nip's Breakfast is the place—it's a friendly spot, and Nip's a pistol. I first met Nip early one morning before the sun came up. Logger Bob introduced me, and Nip looked me up and down. I smiled, held out my hand, and when she didn't shake it, I took it back and put it in my pocket. She weighed all of eighty pounds and had an easy confidence—the queen in her throne room.

"You a logger?" she asked, perhaps not seriously. Probably not. I couldn't tell.

"Interested in logging," I said.

"Well," she said, stabbing her thumb and rolling her eyes at Bob, "what the hell are you doing with him?" And then she hooted and the rest of the place erupted into an egg-spraying laughter that left Logger Bob a little sullen for the rest of breakfast.

This is a good place to find a logger if you need one, although some loggers have Web sites now, and there's a registry of certified loggers kept by the Timberland Owners Association and the County Extension Service. Many loggers have small ads in the yellow pages, but get most of their work by word of mouth. Others lose work by word of mouth; depends on the logger.

The timber companies employed the vast majority of loggers until the Great Depression. After that, the business model shifted to primarily private contractors and it's not likely ever to go back. The timber industry doesn't own any land in New Hampshire anymore, and doesn't care to—there's no real profit in operating a closed industrial loop anymore; everything is outsourced, and if they could somehow contract loggers from Bangalore, they probably would. They barely operate any mills here these days.

Loggers work for themselves and, for reasons that will become obvious, they prefer it that way. Most loggers work in crews of two—a feller who cuts and trims the trees and a skidder operator who hitches the logs and drags them out of the woods and down to the landing. If it's a firewood operation, as opposed to a saw log or pulp wood job, then there's usually a third cutter turning big logs into short logs, and then splitting them so that they fit into the stove.

Unlike the home-cooked coziness of Nip's, the bar was plain, warm, and dark, more like a clubhouse in somebody's basement. I was alone that day—the older loggers get, the less you see of them in the bar rooms. Bob goes straight home to catch the last run of the day up at Cannon Mountain in the winter, he goes to yoga twice a week, and when the snow is gone he rides his bike up and down the mountain roads we live on. Bob's a physical specimen in better shape than most men half his age.

I remembered one of my first visits to this place, almost twenty-five years ago. I usually went to the other bar in town, the hippie bar, which is now an office condominium. This was the redneck bar; lots of people went back and forth between the two, there were no hard rules about it, and everybody was friendly. It was winter, the air was steamy, almost tasty, and my eyeglasses immediately fogged over. I felt greasy, my hair was painted flat on my head, and my ears burned hot and, if they looked like everyone else's, were bright red. As was my nose. Sliding into a chair up against the wall across from the bar was the perfect, quiet little spot for me, like slipping beneath the ground into a cozy fallout shelter just as the bombs began to fall.

The bar was half full, and after nodding and saluting our hellos to people we didn't really know, we sat to drink flattish draft beer. I could have ordered a bottled beer, and created yet another distinction between my colleagues and myself, but I was already walking that delicate line between nuisance and fool with two out of three of these guys. I didn't want to make things worse.

They fumbled with cigarette packs and lighters as they smoked and took long pulls on their beers. We were so tired that nothing seemed interesting enough to actually discuss. No one spoke; I was quiet because my throat hurt from breathing exhaust fumes and screaming at the top of my lungs all day. They were more communicative: they grunted, shrugged, and laughed conspiratorially now and then, probably at me.

Car racing was on the TV; a guy in the corner with a ponytail and jailhouse tats up and down his arms played video poker. This wasn't *Cheers,* nobody yelled our names as we came through the door. But that isn't to say we were unknown. Six of the seven guys at the bar were loggers or sometimes-loggers. They all knew one another's finances, romances, and eccentricities, down to the ugly details. Everybody knew who was a good guy and who would steal you blind. Most guys fell somewhere in the middle.

Three of the loggers at the bar were members of a well-known, if not well-regarded, multigenerational clan of Brush Cats—all sipping beers in the shadows, and ruminating over the next day's job. Logging is usually a family business, but fewer young people than ever are entering the life in the woods. Their folks advise them against it. They say there's no future in it. And while that may not necessarily be true for everyone, it was for these guys.

The seventh drinker at the bar was a used-to-be logger who still told plenty of war stories, suffered excruciating, chronic lower-back pain, and now made his living as a real estate broker. He drank Heineken and played dice. That dude might steal you blind.

I reached into my wallet and extracted the four lottery tickets I'd bought at the gas station that morning when I met them. I happened upon the three of them gassing up a pickup with Vermont plates. One of them hoisted a couple of full jerry cans into the bed of the truck and I could see chainsaws back there. I asked him if they were going logging—he gave me a well-deserved dumb look. I asked if I could tag along. He glanced at the others, their eyebrows rose with their shoulders, and then they nodded okay.

Their eyebrows rose in the same way when they spied the tickets. I passed them around the table with proper solemnity, as if they were secret orders from the High Command. Top prize was ten thousand dollars—not a fortune by any means, but the small jackpot improved the odds. Still, we all knew we had a better chance of spontaneously combusting or marrying into the British royal family than we had of winning a nickel off one of these bad boys. But scratching a ticket is a moment of possibility that triggers the production of pleasurable neurochemicals for some people. These are the same people who buy Megabucks tickets and carry them around in their pockets as talismans that might, on either Wednesday or Saturday every week, deliver them from their current circumstances and into a dream of unearned comfort.

The loggers I sat with were realists; they harbored no illusions about breaking the bank. What they wanted was a buffer against the next economic slump, injury, or unexpected equipment repair. Still, this was a huge chunk of change for these guys, enough for a down payment on a house, or a new pickup, or maybe finally build that in-law apartment so the wife's mother can move in. Think about that: enough money to make your wife love you again.

This was a long time ago, and I was just trying to learn to fell a tree properly in the event that I ever owned any property. Which didn't seem likely at the time, but I also knew I wasn't going to be a logger, partly because I didn't want to, but mostly because I didn't have it in me. Mark finished scratching his first; he stripped it quickly with a gray and greasy right thumbnail. The curl of his lip and the shake of his head said it was a loser.

"Zip," he said, throwing the spent ticket on the table next to the nearly empty pitcher. Jim, too, was a loser, and smiled resignedly. Mike, the third guy at the table, made a big show of using a "lucky" 1969 penny—cherished because it was minted the year his father came home from the war. Mike came up empty, too. I was last and scratched mine with my buck knife, scraped it really—I think that might have been the first time I actually used it for something other than just opening and closing it, or sharpening it for no good reason.

It was a ten-dollar winner, and Mark looked at me as if I were running an ass-backward shell game on them. He grabbed the ticket from my hand and said, "Found money buys." And off he went to the bar.

"Good thing somebody's buying," Mike said. "I'm a joke until the mill settles up." Wood mills are generally known for paying bills in a timely fashion. It's the prices they pay that loggers gripe about. Mike said they'd skated past the magic thirty-day mark with him; they swore it was a mix-up, and it probably was.

Mark ordered shots, and the bartender knew what that meant. It wasn't served as you'd expect—in a shot glass, a single swig. Instead, the Jack Daniels came neat in Manhattan glasses; he knew from experience on both sides of the bar that running a 70 cc chainsaw all day, every day, gave most men a palsy powerful enough to spill good sipping whiskey from a shot glass.

Alcohol and logging have a long and inextricable history. For instance, logger wisdom says to never-ever start a job on a Friday; if you do, everything will go wrong, stuff will break, people will get hurt, and you'll definitely lose money on the deal. Even if it's after dark on a Thursday when you finish the last job, if you want to work the next day, you have to get your skidder over there, cut a tree, and drag it out of the woods and onto the landing. It's a rule—not a law, but not merely a guideline, either. It's understood that to ignore principles is to invite mischief for which you'll receive no sympathy, only scorn and laughter.

This isn't peculiar to loggers. In Ghana, in West Africa, for instance, the ocean is closed on Tuesday; boats are forbidden to go out or come in. No exceptions, including births, deaths, and shark attacks. The practice is meant to give the ocean a rest, to honor the Big Blue as the giver and taker of life. People tell stories of fishermen who tried either to embark or to return on a Tuesday, and who drowned in inches of water, or were eaten by sea monsters. Many more were simply never heard from again. In logging, the rule about never starting a job on Friday isn't like that. It's about getting drunk on payday and messing things up.

The traditional Friday liquid lunch is a six-pack of beer. Some guys might get fancier, but none that I know. The young Brush Cats seldom pass on an opportunity to kick it, and plenty of the old-school guys are straight-up alcoholics who never say no. Friday drinking has no imprimatur on- or off-site. If you get hurt and the hospital says there's alcohol in your blood, then Workers' Comp tells you that your compound fracture is your problem.

Despite all the bad things that can come of it, with the aid of flasks and dented Coleman coolers, the Friday imbibing sometimes continues onto the woodlot and through the afternoon. When that happens, sure enough, before you know it, equipment is breaking, people are getting hurt, and money, according to the accountant, is lost. In the strictest terms, it's not exactly a curse— it's more like cause and effect.

True, on a new job no one has the lay of the land yet, and there's rigging to be done, and lots of trees need to come down all at once in order to stage the operation, making the chances for disaster better than usual. Add a case of beer to bone-deep fatigue and infinite uncertainty, and you've got a full-blown litany of problems. Some bosses tried not working Fridays at all, only to find guys drinking Thursday afternoons instead. As part of their due for living and working out on the edge, some people simply insist upon their forbidden rituals.

The generally accepted lore goes back two centuries to when most loggers were hired by lumber companies and lived in logging camps deep in the woods, where they worked like machines before there were machines to do the work. When they weren't humping trees out of the woods, they ate like bears, and smelled like bears, too. They were wild animals, some said, and hence the name Brush Cat, which the lumbermen wore with some pride, and not much irony.

When the Brush Cats came to town they had wads of cash in their pockets, and knew exactly what they wanted. Down on Skid Row they usually found a bar and a brothel to set up shop in. Among regular folks it created quite a reputation for the Brush Cats, and some still do their best to keep it alive. But the truth is that modern logging is a job like any other, and what sets it apart are its opportunities for death and disfigurement that aren't available in other jobs.

Alcohol was wisely prohibited at these remote logging camps. There's no doubt that forced sobriety saved a lot of lives, and even more limbs, but it rubbed most loggers the wrong way. Telling a man what to do is the first step to telling him what to think. And nobody tells a Brush Cat what to think, unless he has a whole night to argue and fight about it.

We drank up and headed out as we came in—none the wiser or much richer for a full day's work. The next day they moved to a new job harvesting big pines somewhere on Sugar Hill; it was a new milieu full of tricks and dangers, a giant puzzle. It's rocky and steep, and trees are unpredictable when they fall at odd angles. Setting up and then safely and profitably executing a job like this one is a challenge of proportion and consequence that few of us ever face—much less on a daily basis. Logging is more than a job, in the same way as being a soldier, or a disaster relief worker, is more than a job—it's demanding, sometimes excruciatingly so, yet generally underappreciated. For the people who do it because it's important, it's the best job they ever had, and the only one they ever wanted. That was a long time ago, and I haven't seen those guys since. Maybe the work's better over in Vermont.

2

WOODCHUCKS, BRUSH CATS, AND PENCIL MONKEYS

There's nothing that keeps its youth,
So far as I know, but a tree and truth.
Oliver Wendell Holmes

 Down the years I often heard independent loggers called Brush Apes, though the origin of this nickname seems to be lost in history. I did find out, vividly, that Brush Apes don't like that name. This was unknown to me for much of the writing of this book. In fact, *Brush Ape* was the original title. I guess I was vaguely aware that anything that metaphorically referred to a particular group of people as some kind of ape probably wasn't a compliment, but I had no idea how offensive it was. The book was peppered with the term and that had to change. Thank goodness for Ctrl F.

Some, those who live in rented trailers and work the firewood pile cutting eight-foot logs into eighteen-inch lengths all day long, are known as Woodchucks, but again, they're not really crazy about the designation. If you're going to call them anything but loggers you should choose your words carefully. But I don't like woodchucks, the rapacious vermin—not the people—so I avoid thinking of loggers or anyone else in those terms. It makes me want to shoot them with a BB gun, or at the very least snag them in a Havaheart trap and dump them off over in Vermont. Broadly applied, "woodchuck" is northeastern for "redneck." As in, if you use a chainsaw for finish carpentry around your house, you might be a woodchuck.

In early March, Logger Bob and I were in a small woodlot out in Easton, cutting and skidding one-hundred-foot pasture pines out before the state Department of Transportation shut down the roads to loggers. I was late, and he was on his knees trying to tighten the chains on his skidder.

"I knew you'd show up as soon as I was done," he said. "I dubbed around for nearly an hour, figuring you'd roll up and help me with this. Then I just had to get to it. Here, hold this piece of goddamn chain a minute."

He had to have everything on the landing for his trucker, or the road ban could tie up a couple of thousand dollars' worth of wood for who knew how long. As the weather warms, the roads soften when the ice in the soil beneath them melts. The Department of Transportation says that logging trucks break up the roads during these conditions and therefore can't operate.

Garbage trucks, oil trucks, and milk trucks can all use the roads, but the loggers, dump trucks, and anybody pulling a big piece of equipment are verboten.

As far as Bob was concerned, it was a case of "They build the roads like shit and then blame the loggers for busting them up."

I was watching Bob, trying to learn to hitch a rig of logs with grapple and pull them out of the forest on a skidder. But still I have no idea how he does it. The grapple is exactly like those games at the beach or at Wal-Mart, where the goal is to maneuver a three-fingered mechanical claw down into a pile of stuffed animals, clutch one, and carry it up to the prize shoot. It's nearly impossible for me, but every time my son does it he snags something. His first was when he was five years old, and now that he's nine, he doesn't want the prizes; he knows he can beat the machine as easily as tie his shoes, so he's lost interest. Bob's played the games and thinks they're stupid, too, but he runs his skidder's grapple like a robotic arm picking flowers. It has only two fingers, more like pincers, and he controls them with great precision.

He cut two big pines at the end of small skid roads he made off the main road in from the landing. They're built on the bias into the woods, like streams to a river. "Dendritically," Bob says, "like a tree. The pattern gives you the access to the maximum number of trees while doing the least damage to the forest. No damage if you do it right. The lines move at natural angles, opening up sunny spots for the remaining trees. This is forest management. The landowner said to me, 'You can't even walk around in there; what good are woods you can't at least visit?'"

The white pine is the only five-needled pine in the North-east and isn't as resinous as many other varieties. Woodworkers love the white pine for its straight grain and soft, easy-to-work-with wood. These were pasture pines—indicated by their low branches. The branches detract from their value somewhat be-cause the boards they yield are what we call knotty pine.

Bob cut the first one in the time it took me to follow him up the skid row. He was driving five miles an hour, I was walk-ing three miles an hour, and we went only a quarter of a mile. So I was right on his six. Still, by the time I charged to the sound of the chainsaw, he'd already felled the pine and was zipping it clean. I was making notes about this when he was gone again, and as I walked over to where he was ready to drop another, I tripped on some slash and fell on my face in the muddy, green-gray slush. Then I heard the tree crack and the canopy whoosh through the forest and I was sure it was going to land on me. My new name, whether I survived or not, would be Stupid Fuckin' Jack. I've seen it happen before. But it didn't hit me. It landed twenty feet away, and in these tight and overgrown woods, that's like two city blocks.

As I rolled over and scrambled to stand up before Bob saw me, I heard a squawk and looked up. Staring down at me was a gray jay, also known as a Whiskey Jack. My friend Peter calls it the Camp Thief, because they'll snag anything that's not an-chored down—a hot dog off the grill, a sweaty bandana, a bag of gorp. This meant that there are some spruces around, too, be-cause the gray jay prefers the scaly spruce bark to the smooth white pine. This is for a very good reason—the gray jay over-winters in the coniferous forest, surviving on food that it gathers and sticks to the spruce with its extraordinarily sticky saliva. As winter wears on, they survive on this spit-slathered cache of food and seem none the worse for it.

The gray jay—which is actually a variety of crow but looks to me like a chickadee on steroids—lays its eggs in early March, so by mid-April—May at the latest—their young will have lost their sooty-colored down and will start flying and foraging on their own. If you insist on spending the winter here, you have to start early—whether it's collecting firewood, bugs, or berries, it's all the same. The gray jay is an inquisitive bird and seems almost tame at times. This one sat there looking at me as if I were the clumsiest beast on the planet. I certainly was the clumsiest beast in those woods.

Bob limbed a hundred-foot tree in three minutes, jumped in the skidder, put the grapple to the butt end, and dragged it forward fifty feet or so until it was perpendicular to the tree he'd cut previously. Then he laid that butt end on top of the other so it created a ninety-degree angle, backed up a bit and grabbed both trees with the grapple above where they intersected, squeezed the tines shut, and drove forward. The trees shimmied together to move in parallel, and as he rounded the slight corner in the skid road, the narrow end of the second tree whipped around like Godzilla's tale and I had to jump in the air, as if I were skipping rope, so it wouldn't snap both my ankles off. "Keep your eyes open," Bob warned. As I said, he's the pro—any screwups were on me. He prefers to work alone for this very reason. Other people are unpredictable, and it's hard enough to cut trees without worrying if some dunderhead is standing precisely where he shouldn't be.

"There are two generations of trees in here," Bob told me, ". . . the oldest being probably sixty-five years old." Veteran logger and businessman Bob Peckett, no relation to Logger Bob, remembers when this whole valley was pasture. He's eightysomething, and when he was ten years old, he helped hay this area. It hasn't been logged since. "There were some dubbers in here— there's their cable over there, thank God I didn't hit it when I cut the brush. They just left it behind; see it blend in? I don't know what they were logging with, some kind of doodlebug probably, like an old Model A converted to skidding. And they just dubbed around here; you see the old stump? But I'm basically the first one in here, and the different generations of pine are completely different trees. You can see these here where they thinned them out, they grew pretty well. But then there are the bigger ones with the shittier tops, they're more like pasture trees, the branches come all the way to the ground. They're all bound up with one another; you can see the mortality, fighting each other for the sunlight. Blister rust, doubles, all kinds of shit to contend with. Once I get rid of those, it'll be just woods trees after that. There are some bigger, nicer ones I've been working down the back, but I won't finish now.

"This is my last day today because of the road ban. Even though it's cold out. The asshole engineer from Concord just looks at the calendar, picks up the phone, and tells the guys up here to post the signs. Doesn't even bother to drive up here and look. I should be able to go here next week, but no. That's the Department of Transportation for you. I was working by the state shed up near the Notch, so while I was there I cut the dead trees along the edge of the road. A guy comes running out of the state shed yelling, 'What are you doing to my overtime trees?' Overtime trees, I said. What the fuck, these are dead trees, they're hazards. A guy got killed in the notch by a falling tree; another guy on a motorcycle got killed over on the Kancamagus by one. These things are dangerous, they blow down all the time. But the state guys like to keep them where they are, hoping they'll get called out in the evening to cut one up, push it to the side, takes an hour, and they get paid four hours minimum. I told him: they're dead trees, you got to cut them, and he says, 'You can't cut all the dead trees, there's too many.' What the fuck? We built the Hoover Dam, put a man on the moon, but you can't cut all the dead trees along the road before they land on somebody's car? This is what I'm dealing with, these are the kind of people making decisions that affect my life."

Driving the skidder, it turns out, is a lot easier than parallel-parking my Volvo—that is, if you can get used to a stick instead of steering wheel, like in a jet fighter or a Stanley Steamer. Plus, it has a knuckle in the middle and wraps prehensile-like around large objects, making maneuvering the woods possible. For some people. There was Hoppy, a guy Logger Bob worked with, who chose the most challenging skid rows possible in the woods. Up and over rocks, down gulleys with sharp turns at the bottom. He once flipped his skidder twice in two days at the very same spot. In fact, the second time he had an extra tree on the load to prove that it could be done. It couldn't. Bob once found Hoppy at the landing one morning looking especially cranky. "I think some goddamn kids might have been messing with my machine," he said. "Well, Christ, Hoppy," Bob said, "what could kids do to it that you don't?"

When we had a full load at the landing, and all the equipment was shut down so the woods were quiet, Bob looked at me as earnestly as anyone ever has and said, "Any chance you could change the name of this book? *Brush Ape* just isn't very nice. I didn't want to say anything, but most guys would consider that derogatory."

I asked an ex-logger, David Pickman, if there were overly negative connotations with the term *Brush Ape*. "Duh," he said.

"I just don't want to seem like a dick about it," Bob explained. "But nobody is going to appreciate that title."

"I kind of like it though," I said. I've always liked apes. I was raised with monkeys. And I realize monkeys aren't apes, but I have an understanding, if not an affinity, with simians. Except the spider monkey who was as tall as I was, in love with my mother, and hated my guts. He once jumped on my father's shoulders, locked his spindly legs around his neck, grabbed hold of his ears, and bit his bald pate so hard that Dad ran through the neighborhood screaming, "Mary, Jesus, and Joseph, somebody get me my goddamn gun!" It's a good thing he was a cop or people might have talked.

I'm not in any way comparing loggers to apes. No, no, no. Sure, they share a similar habitat and reputation for elusiveness, but the smallest, oldest logger I know could kick my ass for calling him an ape. And he might. Not that he should. I use the term *Brush Ape* with great respect: it has dignity and strength.

"It's a good title," I told Bob.

"Fine," he said. "Then I'll call you Pencil Monkey from now on." And I knew he would.

Bark Eater is another old-timey name for a logger, not a slur, necessarily, but hardly a compliment. It's descriptive, but not very dignified—certainly not "Guardians of the Forest," as Bob suggested. I settled on *Brush Cat,* which can also be found in John T. Labbe and Lynwood Carranco's excellent *A Logger's Lexicon.* Brush Cat: Lion of the Great Northern Forest.

Bob Santy (not to be confused with Logger Bob) and his younger brother, Rick, are exemplary North Country Brush Cats. They're old-school businessmen—do what they say, say what they do. You don't need a contract with these boys—they're honest and fair and fun to have around. That about says it all for me as far as company goes. Smart is high on my list, too. And every good logger I've ever met is as smart as a whip—in fact, every logger I've worked with is a better logger than I am a writer. And being a logger is a much harder job.

I gathered a gang of loggers one night—like many other nights—over beers and dinner in the back room at the Oasis Restaurant in Littleton. As good-naturedly as possible, they lamented the inconceivable stupidity of the federal government, shoddy equipment, the price of fuel, and the short, wet cutting season here in the "Pacific Northeast" this year. And last year. And the year before that.

Logger Bob was the most adamant, which is to say, pissed off.

"What, we used to get into the woods what, eight, nine months a year. Now it's three. Three fucking months of work? Thank Gawd for that gawddamn storm. Without all that blow-down there'd be no frig'n work. I made ten grand just doing storm damage cleanup."

All of them shook their heads in agreement, except Rick, who nearly spit his beer into his fried clams.

"Jesus H. Christ, Bob," he said. "You're not telling me you charge people that much for limbing?"

"Tree surgery," Logger Bob corrected. "And I did a lot of it and I charge the going rate. Anybody who wants to climb a broken tree and cable it, or cut it, fifty or sixty goddamn feet in the air with a chainsaw, is free to. Otherwise, they can call me."

"How do you live with yourself?" Rick laughed. He's big and broad-shouldered, laughs easily, and takes no shit.

"How am I going to live otherwise?" Bob said, a little defensively. But he was right, and all of them, including Rick, shook their heads in agreement.

Twenty years ago, working in the woods was a six-to-eight-month job. But development killed the goose—where there once were dry woodlots you could log in the summertime, there are now houses. Between 1970 and 2006, the population of New Hampshire nearly doubled, from 730,000 to 1.3 million. That's a lot of buildings where there once were woods. Consequently, the number of available woodlots has dropped precipitously. Fewer woodlots, fewer jobs, fewer loggers. Before the great sprawl reached New Hampshire, the average logger had work scheduled two years in advance, and some large woodlots he worked every year on retainer. Now, if a logger has two jobs ahead of the one he's working on, he's lucky.

The ones who hung on and worked smart could still make a decent living—fifty thousand or sixty thousand dollars a year until recently. But then the winters got warmer—often with more snow—so the wetlands that should freeze over so that they can be logged, don't. Again, fewer woodlots, fewer jobs. Loggers who made themselves sixty thousand dollars in 1999 will be lucky to make half that in 2009.

Bob and Rick are Big Bob Santy's boys, and Big Bob is a legend in these parts. He ran one of the biggest independent logging operations around for decades—had twenty Brush Cats working for him, logging with workhorses instead of skidders for most of his life, harvesting his share of trees from the forest, and then some. He was, as they say, larger than life. He was also larger than most human beings. He started in the woods as a youngster, wielding a cross-cut saw to fell trees, yarding giant logs by hand onto a horse hitch to skid them out of the woods. And even when chainsaws came along, they were as big and bulky as a snowblower with a blade—run one of those eight hours a day for a couple of decades and you definitely don't need to go to Jazzercize after work. Big Bob was one of those guys who, if you cut him down the middle, the halves would run in opposite directions just to get more done.

Some wormy little bugger whose name doesn't need to be mentioned here because, according to Bob, he doesn't deserve the notoriety, once taunted Rick on the main street of Lisbon, New Hampshire, for reasons unremembered. Gave him the finger, called him an unspeakable name, and then skedaddled inside the Lisbon Police Department for sanctuary. It was a long-standing dispute and probably seemed like a can't-lose plan to a guy dumb enough to do something so dangerous in the first place. What he hadn't counted on was that Rick Santy was no more afraid of the police than he was of the gormless twit who thought he could hide under their skirts. Rick looks like he's been in the woods felling trees all his life. Big in the shoulders, flat in the stomach, even now in his fifties. He's a large, friendly guy whom other large and unfriendly guys sometimes challenge, and barely live to regret. So Rick walked through the doors of the Lisbon PD, grabbed the shit-bird by the nape of the neck, and gave him a quick beating before the cops had at him with their sticks, and he at them with his fists. Superior numbers and firepower prevailed.

Naturally they locked Rick up, and not in the tidiest or most comfortable cell in the county. Not by a long shot. That was Friday night. By Monday morning, Big Bob said to young Bob, "The cops still got that brother of yours down at the station?"

"Far as I know," says young Bob. "Maybe they got to bring him to court this morning or something."

"Court my ass," says Big Bob. "Christ, they've had him three days already. It's Monday, time to go to work. Go get him."

The first lesson Bob and Rick learned working for their father was that when he sent you after something, you didn't come back empty-handed. That, Bob says, was just inviting some terrible trouble on yourself.

So Bob saunters down to the police station, walks inside calm as a judge, and tells the lone officer at the desk that he wants his brother released.

"No can do," says the officer.

So Bob, who's got big arms and hands, and long legs, and a natural laid-back air of intimidation when necessary, leans in to him and stares him down like he would to somebody being rude to a waitress in a bar.

"You don't get the key and let my brother out of that cell, I'm going to kick your ass. And that's all I'll say."

The officer, all too familiar with the Santy boys and fully cognizant of the better part of valor, opened the cell door and cut Rick loose. There were trees to be felled, and no simple assault charge was going to stand in the way of a Santy and his chainsaw.

I tell this story as an example of the hierarchy of good and evil in a Brush Cat's cosmology. When the woodlot calls, nothing—not a skull-splitting hangover, an unresolved criminal charge, or a nonlife-threatening injury—can stand in the way. It's hard, thankless work, and if you let yourself off the hook for every little excuse that comes along, you'd never be in the woods. You'd just stay in bed. I would, anyway.

Bob is tall and lanky with gray hair and gray beard and blue eyes; a cigarette is usually smoldering around him. He rubbed his chin when I asked him a question: "How old was I on my first job loggin', you mean? My first payin' job? I was thirteen. Doin' it since."

He and his brother Rick ran a good-sized operation for much of the seventies and eighties, but in the nineties they decided to downsize some, take life a little slower, avoid breaking their backs or carving their feet off; there are a lot of reasons to come out of the woods after a lifetime of working in them. One of them, Bob said, "is like the time we had a hundred acres all ready to go to work in—landing built, skids roads all cut. All that was left was the good part when you actually start making some money, and the landowner shows up on-site and says the deal's off. Just like that."

That's a week out of a three-month cutting season that they not only didn't make any money, they lost.

"It's business." Bob shrugs. "You take your lumps and move along."

Rick went into excavating, and Bob drove a log truck. He's a jobber; he'll pick up a logger's load and deliver it to the mill for a price. He drives a GMC, *The General,* big and red and classic. The boom has a grapple with which Bob lifts and stacks logs in the stake bed as neatly as clean underwear in a draw. The first time I met Bob Santy it was this same time of year, and the road bans were on. Bob was complaining that "some old Sugar Hill lady tried to blockade me from driving over a bridge."

A Sugar Hill lady generally denotes an old-money matriarch with a straw hat, wraparound sunglasses, probably a vest of some kind over her cotton shirt, sturdy walking shoes, and an imperiousness that is otherwise found only in inner-city gangs and Victorian royalty. Basically Michael Jackson with a cane and more money.

She's the one who lets the door go in your face at the post office, loves nature and hates people, thinks she's polite because she sends thank-you notes but puts a curse on you if you don't reciprocate, and treats everyone who disagrees with her at town meetings like an impudent child. A regular North Country sweetheart. They like things to look and operate the way they want them to and aren't shy about imposing their aesthetic on others. The Sugar Hill town line is just at the top of my hill, so a lot of

Sugar Hill ladies use my road to get home. One day I found a brand-spanking-new bright green mailbox sitting next to the ancient and rusty one at the end of our driveway. A note inside said, "Happy Spring! Hope you love this!" I didn't.

Sugar Hill ladies also, as far as I can tell, live forever. Which is fine because there aren't many of them, and besides, most of the ladies I know who live in Sugar Hill are absolutely charming. Besides, I don't need the trouble. I'm far more afraid of them than I am of a whole crew-cab truck full of loggers.

There's some history here. Until 1962, Sugar Hill was a village of Lisbon, which sits down in the valley, on the river. Lisbon was a mill town while Sugar Hill was, well, Sugar Hill. Bette Davis lived there, and former U.S. Supreme Court Justice Potter "I can't define pornography, but I know it when I see it", Stewart lived there (and now that he's no longer alive, does that mean American jurisprudence's working definition of *pornography* went with him?); it's the home of Polly's Pancake Parlor, where a stack of pancakes will cost you as much as a full rack of baby-back ribs will at Chili's. When Sugar Hill seceded from the town of Lisbon it immediately became one of the wealthiest towns in the state. The people in Lisbon know why they were rejected.

"So," Bob says, "this Sugar Hill lady is standing there in the middle of the road, just before the bridge, and she hollers, 'You can't drive over this bridge!' As soon as she comes up to my window to chew my ass out some more, I just put it in gear and drove over the bridge. Fuck that. These people are crazy. I don't think I run over her toes; I probably would have heard about it if I had."

Making a living when certain people—abutters, conservationists, and road-ban vigilantes—are opposed to the very idea,
isn't easy.

The Santys are back into logging in a big way. Rick's son
Steve is in his thirties, as big as he is soft-spoken, with a great
wooly beard and clear blue eyes. He had a going career downstate
and all around the country as a millwright. It's precision work
and well paid, but he grew up in the woods, was driving a skidder
before most kids were riding bikes, and the life of the Brush Cat
called out to him. So back to town he came, and he and his father
and uncle put the old band back together again. Steve runs the
whole-tree chipper, which they bought used and use a lot.

I watched him at it one day, standing leeward of the hail of
sawdust and chips flying into the back of a box truck as Steve
maneuvered his grapple onto four or five trees at a time and fed
them into the hopper of the tree chipper like the Juiceman sliding celery stalks into a blender. The giant, toothy drum spins
and grabs them, sucking them inside and grinding them into
little shards of wood in mere seconds. Steve believes that there's
plenty of junk wood in the forest. He points to a giant pile of
red and white pine that he'll chip that afternoon.

"These pine," he pronounces it *poine,* and I find myself doing the same thing more and more, "they would have been good
saw logs someday if they hadn't been blown down. In the old days
these trees just would have sat here to rot, but now there's a demand for them, and I think there's plenty of trees to fill that
demand. Plus, there's no shortage of twenty-four-inch-, thirty-
six-inch-diameter trees, and the way the mills are set up, they
just cut it four times to square it off, cut it in half, and then send

it to resaw for the final dimensions. Seems like a funny question, asking if there are enough trees in the forest, but I know what you mean."

The Santys do it all, the trickier the better—they're guys who can get the most difficult job done without getting hurt and still make a buck at it. Which is a world-class act.

The lot Logger Bob and I were in that day had been partially cut thirty years previously and it was what some loggers prosaically refer to as a "puss job." They cut too much in some places, not enough in others; big pines that should have come down three decades ago but didn't and were now rotting husks, infected by blister rust, worthless.

Bob did have a couple of loads of pulp, which will bring $750 compared to $2,300 a load for good pine saw logs. A well-producing lot will have a mix of four or five loads of saw logs to every load of pulp logs. This woodlot was nowhere near that rich. In fact, it might have been reversed, making for a lot of work, a lot of expense—fuel costs remain constant despite the value of the load—and not much cash in the kitty at the end of the month.

This is a cleanup job, and when the value of the wood doesn't justify the expense of cutting it, the woodlot owner has to pony up the difference. "I used to throw them a bone, no matter what," Bob said. "Landowners expect to make something off a logging job, and arguing the economics of the business with them just wasn't worth the trouble. But now, the margins are so thin I can't afford to worry about my public relations image. But the next time this lot gets logged, the timber will yield a nice profit for everybody. Of course, that's maybe twenty years from now, and people generally don't take that long a view on their land investments. They're patient with their IRAs and 401Ks, sure, and their goddamn stock portfolios, yeah, of course. But timber lots? Nah, they want cash on the barrelhead."

In early 1999, diesel cost 59 cents a gallon; in January 2000, it was up to $2.39 per gallon; today, it's $4.00 a gallon—nearly an 800 percent increase in less than a decade. Every time Bob Santy fuels up *The General*—it gets only three miles to the gallon, so that's at least twice a week—it costs him more than $400.

Staggering fuel costs aren't the only problem. The burst real-estate bubble popped the logging business, too. In 2007, a load of nice pine to be milled into dimensional lumber, or some maple for veneer, brought $3,000. Now you're lucky to get $2,000, and with the ever-rising price of doing business, the profit it turns is down to $750 a load. Or less. Bob can cut two loads a day, no problem, if there's wood to cut, but Bob's productivity or work ethic isn't the problem.

"I can't cut that much today," he said, "because I'm talking to you instead of working—but the cutting time has gone from four solid months just a few years ago to six shitty weeks now. It's a perfect frig'n storm for losing your livelihood. The loggers and the mills saw the real estate crash coming two years before the geniuses on Wall Street did. In 2006, the market couldn't get enough pine to build McMansions; in 2008, nobody's building houses anymore and there's a glut of wood out there. It's Economics 101. When the price drops, it means there's more supply than demand."

It's all about the economic food chain. At the top are those who buy and sell money and produce nothing but profit. Or not. For years, finance companies gave anybody with a pulse a big variable-rate mortgage for a house they couldn't afford, which drove up the value of every other house and made everybody feel like they had inherited a big wad of cash from an uncle they didn't know they had. Hedge funds and investment banks, such as the defunct Bear Stearns, bought the mortgages from lenders because the high interest rates were irresistible, then divided them up and resold them, spreading them throughout the economy like the Ebola virus. Eventually the borrowers couldn't make the payments, and the financial market was undermined. The guys at the top who produce the profits that run the engine ran it too hard. At the micro level, where the chains hit the skid road, how does a Brush Cat plan for next year when he doesn't know what the market will bear, or how much it will cost for the very basics of doing business or how much wood he'll sell? Small operations can't weather too much bust and boom, but a nice quiet, steady, and sustainable demand seems impossible in an industry so closely tied to such speculative markets. It's in the nature of twenty-first-century capitalism— you can't just make money, you have to make it fast. New drugs get approved before they're adequately tested, mortgage borrowers don't need to be vetted, and all presumptions and scenarios are giddily optimistic until, as Bob says, "the shit hits the fan." And it has.

Before the real estate market went tits-up in the river, Bob talked about selling his place—a hundred acres in Sugar Hill with a nice new house on it, great views, lots of privacy. He might have gotten a million bucks for it a couple of years ago. But now, who knows? It'll still bring a nice chunk of change, but once Bob gets everything paid off, there may not be enough left for a forty-nine-year-old guy to retire on. So it seems he, like thousands of others, is locked into a dying way of doing business. Pretty soon, being a logger will mean you work a feller-buncher for some big mechanized outfit, or you chip trees for biomass and nothing else. This is a big step down in the hierarchy of logging. Bob and any other talented Brush Cat regard chipping as the meatball side of the business. Oh, sure, if you've got a whole-tree chipper, running the boom can be fun, nobody's denying that, but it's hardly what makes logging interesting. Hell, *I* chip every year. Of course, in order to cut the trees to chip I can't keep the chain on a saw for more than ten minutes, or manage to cut more than two trees without getting my bar hopelessly wedged—but I chip like a champ. Because it's easy and boring—exactly what a Brush Cat hopes to avoid in the woods.

Logging as a way of life as opposed to just a job is all about facing the challenge, planning your attack, and executing it well. "You know," says Bob, "when one of those big fat green-headed horseflies chases you, biting you and buzzing in your ears, *fucking tormenting your ass all day long,* and then you finally figure out his moves, match his speed, outwit the little bastard and smack him hard on your leg or your arm so his guts all squish between your fingers—that's an accomplishment."

3

SAW

*I like trees because they seem more
resigned to the way they have to live
than other things do.*
   Willa Cather

 My father never let me cut the grass with
the power mower, not even when I was in college.
He regarded me as "accident-prone," which was a
nice way of saying "stupid." And in a power-tool context, I
won't argue with that. I'll also admit that I've never improved
my mechanical skills much beyond the ability to zipper my
coat without help. But that very same stone-cold ignorance
drives me to do the things I shouldn't, because what would life
be without that?

So I grew up around no power tools. Zero. My father didn't
have a table saw, a skill saw, a jigsaw—not any kind of saw. I

vaguely remember a rusty hacksaw hanging on a nail in the basement, but I had no idea what it was for; it was probably there when my folks bought the house.

He knew better than to have anything too dangerous around, because if I'm accident prone, I inherited it. Cases in point: from my earliest memories, our house was full of guns—yet, when I was in high school, my father shot himself while deer hunting. Which isn't easy. A couple of years before that, a horse fell on him and broke his legs. When he was in the navy, a motorcycle accident in Tokyo landed him in the hospital for nearly two years. "They drive on the wrong side of the road," he told me.

So I come by this honestly. When I was seventeen, I seized the engine in his car by driving it at high speeds and never checking the oil. He said, "It's a good thing your head is screwed on, because you'd work nails loose." But I knew he was talking about both of us. I mean, he's the one who taught me to drive.

And in that Freudian paternal framework I came by my interest in chainsaws. They were the most verboten item on the list of things I was not to mess with. As a teenager I could ride motorcycles, roam the streets of Boston until the wee hours, go off hunting with as many guns as I wanted, even work as a security guard in a cat-food factory. Once, after signing my report card, my father encouraged me to join the service after high school and go to Vietnam, even though the war was over. Nevertheless, wood chippers, meat grinders, and, most of all, chainsaws(!) were as off-limits as heroin and voting Republican. Maybe more so.

So I love/hate chainsaws. As do most loggers. Not that I'm a logger; I've never made a living at it. My chainsaw doesn't even have a name, or a gender. I also don't treat it like a Stradivarius. Of course, I put fewer hours on my saw in a year than most loggers do in a week. It's the tool of their trade, so they can be forgiven their fetishism. I saw it as something to be conquered—which, from the outset, was a bad plan. Every Brush Cat knows that the more kindness and respect you show a chainsaw, the less likely it is to bite you.

I will say that chainsaws are real timesavers. Like nuclear weapons. In the same time it takes me to get dizzy and clutch my chest using a bow saw, I can cut 5,000 percent more trees with my Dolmar. Maybe it's saving me from a coronary or massive stroke. Truth told, for the weekender, using a chainsaw is like saying "Beetle Juice" three times—a calculated risk with a strong potential to go terribly wrong.

Modern chainsaws aren't the man-eaters that their fore-bearers were. We can thank Ralph Nader for that. Before consumer-protection laws, you were safer rattlesnake handling drunk and naked than you were running a chainsaw all day. But in this era of OSHA and more personal-injury lawyers than there are personal injuries, chainsaws come equipped with a full complement of safety features. Chain guards, for instance, are very nice: they keep the chain—that sharpened piece of metal whipping around the bar at 1,000 RPM—from flying off and wrapping itself around your leg and mistaking it for a different kind of limb. Brake bars, mounted on the front of the saw to halt the chain from spinning if (when) the saw kicks back at you, are also a great innovation. They add a little weight to the saw but don't impede its power or speed. Still, I've seen loggers get out a wrench and tear the brake bar off.

Safety chains are effective but contain a paradox. They're standard equipment on consumer-grade rigs, and have an extra superscripted link designed to keep the saw from kicking back into your crotch or onto your face and seriously affecting your social life forevermore. And that's good. The inherent contradiction of the safety chain is that while it decreases the likelihood of one's body coming into contact with the business end of the bar, it also makes the safest way to cut a tree—the open-notch method—all but impossible.

The open-notch method is the safest way to cut, and that's how I was taught by Spencer Larabee, logger extraordinaire. Spencer runs a tight logging operation and teaches on the side. He's an open-notch evangelist, claims it saves many lives, and I'm sure he's right. I've cut trees traditionally, with a big deep notch in the front and a hinge in the back. I find it difficult to predict which way a tree will fall using this method, and that's an important detail that goes beyond safety. You don't want to drop a tree on top of a tree that you want to cut, or for it to get caught up in a tree, or destroy a nicely maturing young tree that you could harvest in a few years. And, of course, you don't want it to fall on you or your friends.

To cut open-notch, you first make a bore cut in the center of the tree at a 180-degree angle to the clear-fall path you've chosen. Cut the bore hole to the back of the tree, leaving a one-inch hinge. Next, in line with the bore cut, carve a long, shallow wedge two inches deep (no closer than an inch from your bore cut), then finish your wedge by cutting straight down the face of the tree at a 70-degree angle. You want to avoid what Spencer calls "bypass," which is when your wedge cut bypasses your bore cut, making them a single cut and compromising the integrity of the hinge—which is all that is holding the tree up. Bypass increases the chance of the tree barber chairing—that is, falling over backward on you. The beauty of this method is that when you're ready to fell the tree, you need only touch the hinge with your chainsaw to finish the cut. Don't worry, I didn't get it the first time it was explained to me, either.

But when I watched Spencer demonstrate the cut, it made perfect sense, and I was smitten, mildly euphoric, actually excited about cutting trees. I realize that this sounds odd, but I'd been at this awhile and until that moment it had been like riding a motorcycle without ever getting out of second gear. But this was so simple and so seemingly safe that I immediately developed a confidence with a saw in my hand that I'd never had before.

The open-notch cut isn't only safer, it reduces the amount of wood wasted by deep-wedge cuts, as well as fiber pull—that's when the xylem yanks up out of the tree as it falls, leaving spikes on the trunk and a damaged butt end on the log.

Here's the rub with the open-notch cut. To make your bore cut through the trunk of the tree, the saw needs a lot of grabby traction on the underside of the tip. But it's that same motion in reverse that causes a saw to kick back at you when you touch the top side of a running saw on a piece of lumber. The safety chain is designed to impede that motion. So, while it won't kick back as easily or as forcefully, it also won't let you cut the tree in the safest manner possible. I didn't know this at the time, and was disappointed that it wasn't as easy as it looked. I struggled with it, cut all the trees I was supposed to, but the other guys were having a much easier time of it. I figured it was just another case of my being a hobbyist and their being the real deal. At an ear-lier logging class, one on building bridges and culverts, I ap-proached the forester from the U.S. Forest Service who taught it and said, "Um, I was wondering if I could interview you later. I'm not really a logger, I'm writing a book about logging."

"Really?" he said. "You blend so well."

I asked Spencer, my new safety guru, what he thought I was doing wrong.

"You got to get rid of that chain and get yourself some-thing a little more aggressive. Or you might start with simply sharpening the one you have. Looks like a dull saw to me." So, yeah, as I said, I'm a dope.

Consumer-sized saws, like mine—50 cc is plenty big for me—come standard with safety chains. The assumption here (I'm guessing) is that anyone who goes to a big-box store and buys a Chinese-made chainsaw doesn't know how to cut a tree safely or otherwise, anyway. They also probably don't do much cutting, either—a limb here, a sapling there around their one-acre lots. So a saw with training wheels is adequate for their purposes—more than enough, actually. The truth is, they should stick to hand-saws, and take a break whenever they get short of breath or tight in their chests. They'll get a little exercise and might avoid a lot of bloody grief.

When a real logger with two brain cells to rub together uses a chainsaw, he wears steel-toed boots, Kevlar chaps, a hard hat with a metal cage around his face, and solid ear protection. I al-ways do, and frankly, in that full getup, I look like one of the Village People. But I've seen the damage that can happen without it, so I can live with my twelve-year-old daughter telling me, "That's quite a look, Dad." Or my nine-year-old son saying, "With that stuff, you look like you actually work." I won't tell you what my wife says.

Before chaps, the emergency room doctors preferred loggers wear short pants whenever possible. It avoided having to pick all the tiny threads out of their nasty leg wounds before they could sew them up.

Double ear protection—earplugs and ear cups—is advised, and even that will protect you from only 50 percent of the 90 to 120 decibels that a full-throttle big-ass, pro-class chainsaw puts out. Which is why all loggers over the age of fifty need hearing aids. They don't always have them, but take my word for it— they need them. One guy told me his boss said so many stupid things because he couldn't hear himself saying them.

Logging boots typically have steel toes and high rubber heels to help negotiate the mud one invariably wades through in a woodlot, especially around the landing where the logs are stacked for transport to the mill. This is also the one place on a job where a safety chain on your saw is valuable. Wet and muddy logs are treacherous, and you never know when the chain is going to bind up and make the saw kick. The safety chain's extra links lessen that possibility.

It's a good habit not even to start a chainsaw without the proper body armor, unless you're working on it, which you will be, a lot. But weekenders who wind up in the emergency room are usually wearing sneakers, khaki shorts, and a New England Patriots hoodie. Around here, anyway. Maybe in Atlanta they wear Falcons T-shirts. If you wouldn't wander around Baghdad dressed like a tourist, you shouldn't go into the woods to cut trees dressed like one, either.

In the end, all the best practices a logger can learn might not be enough. One guy I heard about at a logger-safety class got hit on top of the head by a branch falling out of the canopy. He was wearing a hard hat, but still got his bell rung. He called it a day, drove his truck off the landing and up to the road, looked left and then right, and passed out. His neck was broken. The Brush Cat math goes like this: a half-inch-diameter branch falling sixty feet is the equivalent of getting hit by an eight-hundred-pound log. I don't know exactly how that works, but it sounds like it hurts.

As I write this, just yesterday, according to the *Union Leader* newspaper, an experienced logger, a man of fifty, cut a big tree, which bounced unpredictably off the small tree next to it, fell backward, and crushed him to death. He'd been doing it all his life, had no doubt felled tens of thousands of trees, but all it took was one to end it.

So I always wear the Full Monty, even if I'm just zipping out some brush with my saw. But I have no illusions of invulnerability. I feel pretty much like I could be eviscerated or squashed like a bug every moment I'm cutting.

Those are my primal fears. My higher-order problem with the chainsaw is that it's like owning an Italian sports car—if you don't have a personal mechanic, you'd better be handy. It's not that they're more complicated than similar machines, such as lawn mowers and flamethrowers, it's just that if anything is broken, or working badly, it increases your likelihood for an accident.

Fortunately, I have a personal mechanic in the person of Don, the chainsaw dealer who sold me the beast. And he's happy to fine-tune any little problem I sense in it, for fear that I'll cleave my face in half and he'll have to look at my slouching, disfigured visage around town forever. Actually, he's just a very nice guy who takes pity on dopes like me. He and his colleague, Mike, have helped me on many occasions. Frankly, I have trouble changing a tire, and a chainsaw is a bit beyond my skill set. It doesn't have an abundance of moving parts, but all of them are very important.

A high premium is placed on a light saw. If you handle it eight hours a day, the difference between 13.3 pounds and 11.7 pounds adds up. So everything—from the exhaust on the power plant to the tip of the bar—is essential, and if it isn't working properly, you'll know it first. A stalling motor or slipping clutch can make it kick; a bent bar, a weak link, or not enough oil can throw a chain.

It's like a gun—scary, but predictably unpredictable. If you have an accident with one, it's always your fault. You picked it up, you knew what it was, you knew what it could do, and it was in your hands when it did it. Running a chainsaw all day for a living is an extraordinary acceptance of personal responsibility.

One day last spring we had a big blow come through town—seventy-mile-an-hour sustained winds whipped the hundred-foot pines up and down my driveway until they were bowed like daisies after a spring downpour. Before the storm was over, more than a hundred trees around my house were either on the ground or fatally uprooted and in need of euthanizing. So I got out the chainsaw, the chaps, the headgear, the gloves, and my best possible attitude—which in the face of a lot of heavy lifting is about as positive as my attitude on April 15, when I invariably write a big check to the government to cover all the essential services I neither need nor use. And that's exactly how I felt about this chainsaw. Fortunately, I'm a hunt-and-peck typist and don't really need or use all my fingers, either.

Unfortunately, the storm also took a lone and unprotected paper birch next to my house. It was eighty feet tall, but only two feet in diameter. An oak or fir tree that tall would be much bigger at the base. That's why you see paper birches in pairs: they support each other in their shared root system and benefit from each other's mass in windstorms like that one.

I don't mean to be mawkish, or even the least bit sentimental about it, but this tree had personality. It had been there, in that same spot season by season, year after year, growing and thriving while this was all still forest. It was a seedling when I was born, a sapling when Kennedy was president, a tree when the Beatles broke up, a big tree when the Red Sox won the World Series, and now it was dead.

It was a beautiful tree that leaned invitingly toward the stone walkway that leads to the door, almost as if to say, "Come on in." It reminded me of a palm tree, and where palm trees grow is where I'd rather be most of the time.

That precipitous lean is what did it in. It had the misfortune of favoring the same northeasterly direction the wind blew in from that afternoon. When I wandered down the path from my office I saw it—fatally wounded and barely holding on at about a thirty-degree angle from the ground. It was a horse that needed shooting.

I had a freshly sharpened chain on my saw and the first cut I made couldn't have been any smoother or effortless if I'd been using a light saber (although light sabers are much easier to start). The cut caused the butt to crack and snap forward, so its suffering was over in moments. But when I undercut it to finish the job, my saw's bar jammed in the two opposing pieces of wood. After several minutes of trying to nuance the tip out of a ton of convergent push, I started yanking on it only a little less frantically and with more adrenaline-filled energy than I'd use to pull one of my kids out of the jaws of a shark.

Once again, I broke my saw. I pried it out of entrapment with a giant iron bar I keep for just such occasions, gave it a cursory once-over, and restarted it. I'd made two more cuts when the chain came jangling off, dangling from the bar like a limp strand of spaghetti. I try to look on the bright side when these things happen. Without the chain guard, for instance, the chain would have come to rest somewhere in my groin, perhaps snugged up between the cheeks of my arse, before coming to a stop. And that would have been a much worse situation than a half-cut tree.

But now I have to put the chain back on—which isn't like putting a chain on a bike, which is hard enough. I've watched guys put chains back on their saws as easily as they tie their boots, but it's an insurmountable task for me. No matter what I do, how long I work at it, or the number of adjustments I fiddle with, I cannot get the chain back on the saw tightly enough. Or loosely enough. And by the time I stop trying, I'm so worked up and pissed off that I grab a handsaw and attack the tree until I'm worn out to the point of collapse. If the handsaw would cut the chainsaw, I'd cleave that son of a bitch into pieces, too. Then I go into the house and try, once again, to talk my wife into buying a condominium, where, for a monthly fee, they plow the snow, cut the grass, and get rid of any downer trees before you even know they've fallen. We used to live in a condo in suburban Washington, D.C., where a big old pine came down in a storm one day—nearly hit my patio—and sure enough, the association had a crew out there a few days later carving it up and hauling it away. But that's when I was in my thirties; now that I'm fifty, I cut my own wood and yard it around like a beast of burden. What's wrong with this picture?

4

WHOSE WOODS?

We abuse land because we regard it as a commodity belonging to us. When we see land as a community to which we belong, we may begin to use it with love and respect.
Aldo Leopold

In 1915, fresh from slaying them dead in Europe, Robert Frost bought a farmhouse in Franconia and moved his young family here, where they lived from 1915 to 1920, and then nineteen successive summers more. His property abuts mine in the back, but we both have a fair amount of land, making the houses more than a half mile apart. The Frost place is now The Frost Place, a seasonal arts center. The house and grounds are a living museum, an artist-in-residence moves in every summer, poetry workshops and readings absolutely abound, an executive director runs the show, a board runs the risk, and an advisory committee, some of them poets, keeps the pinot noir flowing. Frost would not appreciate all the bustle and clatter, but he'd most certainly admire the effort made in the pursuit of poetry.

The Frost Place is small and utilitarian. It's close to the road, up the hill twenty feet or so, as if on a pedestal. There's a nice porch out front, a homey, woodsy-but-dignified feel inside, and a serviceable old barn out back. I'd tell you exactly where it is, but I'm afraid you might visit. The Frost Place attracts a large following each summer and I've nearly run down more than my share of clueless men in berets who think that because they're in the country, it's okay to wander down the middle of the road engrossed in a chapbook.

Despite the great reviews, Frost decided that World War I was reason enough to move the family Stateside, out of Britain. One day, on a trip to Franconia, they were tooling down Ridge Road, probably in a Model T, and saw the house he wanted. He stopped and, one straightforward sort to another, offered the farmer a thousand dollars for the place. Sounded good. The land is hilly down at that end, full of glacial boulders and wide veins of granite ledge. I have a garden, but it's all raised beds. I wouldn't dream of fighting with that turf. When we first bought the place I tried to till the soil for a garden and nearly lost a foot when the rototiller spun on a rock. And that was in the first thirty seconds. The farmer wanted a better piece of land from which to scratch out a living, and a grand for the old place was a fair deal. Right there in the parlor they came to an agreement.

I shouldn't mention that there were those around town when I first came here in 1984 who remembered Frost. Most said he was a bit of a prick. Of course, they may have read that in any one of a dozen Frost biographies that say pretty much the same thing. Others tell a different version of the farm story—that he stole the property out from beneath the old farmer for back taxes. I never believed it. It was too black-hearted to be true. Frost may have had early-onset curmudgeonliness, but that didn't make him a pirate.

British success had made Frost a phenom at home at a time when real people still read poetry. And he could well afford the farm. In fact, when the Yankee learned who Frost was, through the newspaper, he put the arm on him for a couple of hundred more bucks to seal the deal. Frost paid.

As I said, there's nothing special about The Frost Place, per se. It's all location, the spot in the universe it occupies. Frost and I bought our houses for the same reason: the view—an unobstructed 270-degree vista of the White Mountains with Mount Lafayette up close and dead center. I've climbed Mount Lafayette forty times in the past twenty-five years, most of them before I bought this place. It's a rugged hike no matter which trail you take. I've been up there on the Fourth of July when the summit was so packed it looked like the boardwalk at Hampton Beach. Tens of thousands of people come from all over the world to see it and its environs. I was sitting in the Greenleaf Hut on Mount Lafayette one summer afternoon when two German friends happen to bump into each other at the lemonade cooler. "Oh—mein Gott!" said one. I've been at the summit in the fall, when the surrounding White Mountains and their foothills glowed like a roiling lava flow, and I've been there in the dead of winter, standing with my climbing partner on the peak, barely able to close-haul the wind, picking my way across the mile and a half long Razor Ridge, exposed to anything and everything the day had to offer.

The mountain anchors the east side of a narrow notch—what they call a pass out west; its proximity to the ridge Frost lived on and its unusual beauty draw people to it. Lafayette folds in on itself, cleaving a deep ravine in its lower half that sweeps down nearly two thousand feet into the notch. Its summit is granite variegated by alpine lichens. On a low-pressure day the clouds roll up through Franconia Notch and drip from the summit like warm Marshmallow Fluff. Then they hang heavily in the valley, creating the illusion for those of us living on the eastern slope of Sugar Hill that we're up above it all, looking down on the world.

In his poem "New Hampshire" Frost wrote:

> *I'm what is called a sensibilitist,*
> *Or otherwise an environmentalist. . . .*
> *The more the sensibilitist I am*
> *The more I seem to want my mountains wild. . . .*

But he didn't think they were high enough.

In any case, Frost abandoned New Hampshire in 1939 for Ripton, Vermont, near Middlebury College. Maybe Mount Lafayette lost its allure. Maybe a teaching job at Middlebury for a guy who never finished college was too good a deal to pass up.

He bought a farm house similar to The Frost Place, which is now also a shrine to his memory and work. But in January 2008, thirty local teenagers busted into the place, drank themselves silly, peed and yakked all over the floor, broke windows, burned antique furniture to stay warm, emptied the fire extinguishers all over the rooms full of books, and left. People around here say that's what he gets for moving to Vermont. Actually, Frost said it best:

> *Well, if I have to choose one or the other,*
> *I choose to be a plain New Hampshire farmer*
> *With an income in cash of say a thousand*
> *(From say a publisher in New York City).*
> *It's restful to arrive at a decision,*
> *And restful just to think about New Hampshire.*
> *At present I am living in Vermont.*

Mount Lafayette was originally called Big Haystack (which accounts for Little Haystack nearby) until our forebears made it a memorial to the Revolutionary War hero Marquis de Lafayette. It sits amid the Presidential Range, next to Mount Lincoln and directly across from where the Old Man of the Mountain once hung—nice real estate. Despite this, I have a one-hundred-year-old photograph of Mount Lafayette hanging on the wall of my office in which the scrub growing back from a clear cut around its base and halfway up its north side is clear. A fire may have made things worse. There were many forest fires back then, fueled in large part by the treetops the loggers left in the woods.

I'd been thinking about Frost—his love for this place and my occasional ambivalence—and thinking about what Frost might have done when he was feeling the deep churn of unfilled desire. I imagine that Frost's desires were less venal than mine. In this instance, I was hoping to go to Portsmouth for the night for some beer, music, and maybe, if I got really crazy, a little TV. But another commitment came up, and I was feeling the weight of cabin fever and I thought: *What would Frost do?* I had no real idea, but chopping a tree came to mind. Physical and grunty, it makes you sweaty and tired, and appreciative of your other pursuits.

Naturally, since I'd been lucky on the mountaintop in the dead of winter, a quick jaunt out to the rear acreage of my property seemed like a walk in the park. I'd been laid up for months with a torn IT band in my right knee—I ripped it slipping on a slimy log at a landing in Landaff, and after months of rest and physical therapy—and a newly acquired taste for laziness—I was finally feeling as if I could get around again. Certainly if I wanted to wander down through the woods to The Frost Place in a snowstorm, I was enough of a mountain man not to get lost. It's flat ground and a straight shot through the woods. Without giving it much thought (my first mistake), I grabbed an ax from the shed, and without telling anybody where I was headed (my second mistake), I traipsed off to slay a tree.

I wasn't out to chop just any tree; I was looking for one that *needed* cutting. A big ugly half-burnt-orange, ant-filled balsam probably—a nearly dead wreck that was just begging for it. In the summertime, if you hit one like that, hundreds of ants pour from the trunk. There's always something frightening about a horde, no matter how small they are. And I've never really liked the ants—I have a lifelong territorial dispute with them that paleohistory condemns me to lose. Bernd Heinrich, in *The Trees in My Forest*, writes about studying these tree-eating ants closely and determining that while they can be destructive, they're also stewards over the aphids, which eat other, more destructive insects. That's right, the ants herd the aphids as if they were sheep. Why? Because the aphids excrete a sugary goo from their anuses that the ants are just wild about. He likens it to shepherds drinking goat's milk. I get the analogy, but I think we can all agree that anuses are not breasts. Not even goat breasts. Maybe it's the hardcore mammal in me, but while insects are an integral link of every forest's ecosystem, and tiny mysteries to children and entomologists, to me they're just goddamn bugs.

Since there were a few hundred trees on my property that fit the horse-with-a-broken-leg criteria, I figured I'd find a really egregious one. It was a mission of mercy. The oaks are slowly repopulating the woods, and the towering evergreens slow their progress. Hardwoods are shade resistant, but that doesn't mean they don't like the sun. Clearing out a few overgrown weeds is never a bad thing for the forest.

I'm less likely to cut a tree for no reason than I am to buy more refrigerators than I need. During America's first Great Deforestation in the eighteenth century, Benjamin Franklin wrote that America was "Scouring our Planet . . . making this Side of our Globe reflect a brighter Light to the Eyes of Inhabitants on Mars or Venus." When I first read that, I decided that the stories about Washington, Franklin, and hemp must be true.

But of course, Ben was spot-on. In a single century, thousands of square miles of trees were felled, opening up a patch of sunshine that gave way to new species migrations, wildlife habitats, and human colonization. It was both necessary and sad, as it is when any beast is tamed.

I came by that quote from Franklin on the NASA Web page accompanying a digression analysis of the tree canopy from 1750 to the present. But when I went back to look again, the page was gone. So I did another search and found the full quote, from *Ethnicity and Family Therapy*, by Monica McGoldrick, Joe Giordano, and Nydia Garcia-Preto. It turned out to be a rhetorical question:

> "And while we are, as I may call it, scouring our planet, by clearing America of woods, and so making this side of our globe reflect a brighter light to the eyes of inhabitants on Mars or Venus, why should we, in the sight of superior beings, darken its people? Why increase the sons of Africa, by planting them in America, where we have so fair an opportunity, by excluding all blacks and tawnys, of increasing the lovely white and red? But perhaps I am partial to the complexion of my country, for such kind of partiality is natural to Mankind."

Which is why, despite his retreat to Vermont, when it comes to wise men, I'll take Robert Frost over Ben Franklin. "Fear not being worthy," Frost wrote, "I am a freethinker. I believe in change."

The winter of 2007 wasn't that cold, but we got more snow than we'd seen in previous years. All over the state, schools, big-box stores, theaters, museums, and warehouses were collapsing under the snowload. Most areas got more than ten feet of snow. West Stewartstown, about ninety miles north, got nineteen feet of snow. There were big dumps of powder so deep and fluffy that you could cut a thousand-board-foot tree and lose it in the drifts as it dropped. The loggers literally dug holes around the bases of trees in order to get in there to cut them—try making a hasty retreat from a falling tree under those circumstances. Can't do it.

The snow falling the day I went a-cutting was light and dry, the kind that easily shakes from pine boughs onto your head and down your neck. A couple of hundred yards into the woods, I stopped to wipe the moisture from my glasses and dropped them in the powder. Like magic, they disappeared. They were brand new, cost me five hundred bucks, and I couldn't read or drive without them—so I searched frantically on my hands and knees in two feet of snow for a few minutes until I had to take my gloves off to actually find them. After that, my hands never got warm again. Once, up on Mount Lafayette in February, I made the mistake of bringing an orange to eat. When I was done with it, the juice covered my hands, froze, and stayed that way—I had sticky frozen mitts for the last four miles of the trip. I couldn't stop thinking of that scene in Jack London, in the Yukon, where a trekker loses his glove and realizes it was the turn of fate that would kill him.

As I trudged through the woods I saw a lot of barely standing husks more than deserving of a full frontal assault, but I was looking for the quintessential clean kill—one that gave more life than it took. And then I found it. A ravaged, spindly balsam, ugly from every objective point of view, and bigger than it ought to be. Beneath it, a healthy oak sapling leaned into its ruined trunk, using it as a crutch to stave off the wind and the weight of the snow. Which it needed when it was a seedling; but the oak was a couple of inches in diameter now, and its relationship of

convenience with the balsam had run its course. I cocked the ax
back over my shoulder and addressed the balsam at an angle
from which I could avoid barking the small oak. Just as I was
about to strike, over my shoulder I saw that the ax handle was
cracked (my third mistake), a fatal defect I had missed in my
haste to get out into the woods. It was clear that if I were to lay
into anything more solid than a ripe pumpkin, the ax head
would fly off and, the way my luck was running, bury itself in
my wounded knee. So, after a brief reconnoiter, during which I
found three inches of fresh snow on the brim of my hat, I made
the command decision to postpone the actual tree-felling phase
of the mission and concentrate on returning home.

It wasn't quite dusk, but it was definitely dusky, and naturally since I was on my property I didn't have a headlamp, or
even a penlight. Fortunately, I did have a cell phone, and though
I'd rather have frozen like Otzi in the Austrian Alps than call for
a rescue from my own backyard, I could use it as a light source.

I admit I got off the mark intentionally. I was looking for
the best possible tree to chop, because chopping is hard work
and I wouldn't be doing it again anytime soon. Although I know
these woods well, and they're not that big, or filled with tiger pits
or interdimensional wormholes, I was nonetheless, as we say,
"somewhat lost."

Any idiot could find his way out of these woods in the day-
light, or at night with a light. But I'd stumbled into a mess of
blow-downs and tried to find my way around it. When I stopped
walking to take my bearings, I felt as if I were in a completely
foreign place, a patch of woods I'd never seen before. The glacial
outcroppings were huge and unfamiliar, the lay of the land was

different, and since it was snowing, I couldn't see the mountains anywhere. I was lost. In his diaries, Frost wrote of these very same woods:

> How from politeness to trees I always rounded a circle to the right instead of the left when I got lost in the woods.

So I tried that, and to what end I have no idea.

I should probably have dropped the useless ax, but how ironic would it be if an ax murderer finally found me here in the woods, alone and helpless, and bludgeoned me with my own broken ax? My head certainly isn't much sturdier than a ripe pumpkin. So I yarded it around with me. These, and other thoughts best not shared, streamed through my head. I was panicking. A little. And I was incredibly pissed at myself, which always improves a stressful situation.

Soon, the snow was no longer the problem; the dark was. My fault entirely—night comes early, and this wasn't some unsuspected squall that snuck up on me, either. The snowstorm had been blowing before I'd set out late in the afternoon. And, of course, the sun sets early at this time of year. So it was hard to act surprised. But easy to feel stupid. The philosopher Ludwig Wittgenstein, who wrote about math, the mind, and language—and whom I am not close to ever understanding—said one thing that I do comprehend completely: "Don't try and shit higher than your arse." It's sage advice and exactly what I was thinking as darkness fell.

I tried following my tracks, and while the fresh ones were obvious, those that really mattered—the tracks that actually led somewhere—were filled in by falling, blowing snow. But hey, I wasn't really lost. Uphill not very far was a road; downhill a bit farther was another road. Even if I got turned around completely and missed both, I'd eventually either stumble into my own back-yard or Bob Frost's. But at the moment I was in a gully, unsure of what was uphill and what was down. East, west, forget about it. Taking this walk naked might have made me feel a bit more ridiculous, but not by much. The worst that could happen now is that I would be stuck out in the elements overnight, which wouldn't be a problem if I had my expedition coat and moun-taineering boots on with my balaclava under my hood, my hiking kit including my Leatherman to cut pine boughs to cover myself, some matches to start a fire, a bottle of water, some energy bars, and a light! Sustenance, shelter, fire. That's all what we need. Everything else is for fun. That becomes obvious pretty quickly.

I didn't have anything to stave off the elements. I wore my leather, steel-toed logging boots, a canvas jacket, and a yellow baseball cap from the Dip Net restaurant in Port Clyde, Maine, that my kids gave me for Father's Day a couple of years ago. Be-ing missing all night with my car in the driveway and no note to explain my absence (see above: my second mistake) would cause enough trauma around the McEnany Manse. But oh how I didn't want them to find me frozen stiff wearing that hat. They'd be gone another hour, and usually on those nights I'd be putting dinner on the table as they came through the door. Now my wife was going to have to cook. I sat down under a big old semisnag maple. A snag is a dead tree, a semisnag is mostly dead. I figured misery loves company. Which got me thinking again about my closest, long-dead neighbor, Robert Frost.

"Stopping by Woods on a Snowy Evening"

Whose woods these are I think I know.
His house is in the village though. . . .

Wrong, Bob. These are my woods. And I don't live in the village, I live somewhere right around here. I'm freezing the boys off; how about helping a brother out?

He will not see me stopping here
To watch his woods fill up with snow.

To watch my pants fill up with snow.

My little horse must think it queer
To stop without a farmhouse near
Between the woods and frozen lake
The darkest evening of the year.

He gives his harness bells a shake
To ask if there is some mistake.

What your horse thinks is queer is my house. It's not a farmhouse, it's a five-sided hyperparabola—a house-size blobject. And it spooked the beejesus out of our horse the first time she saw it, too. Do you think you could shake his bells on over here and give me a lift home? Or maybe just to your place? You got any beer back there?

The only other sound's the sweep
Of easy wind and downy flake.

Which describes today—tonight—perfectly.

The woods are lovely, dark and deep,
But I have promises to keep,
And miles to go before I sleep,
And miles to go before I sleep.

And that, presumably, is exactly how you feel just before hyperthermia carries you away to the great MacDowell Colony in the sky.

Hyperthermia is a horrible thing. A couple of winters ago a hiker died over in Bethlehem, just a few miles from here over Mount Agassiz. He camped for the night, not up on a mountain but down in the flats. Still, the temperature dropped to thirty below zero and his sleeping bag was inadequate to spare life in the arctic cold. In the final stages of hyperthermia he imagined that he was on fire and tore his clothes off, running through the woods in an utter panic. They tracked him by the trail of clothing and found him far from his campsite in his underwear, frozen to death. It was a complete accident. There was some speculation that he was despondent and perhaps wanted to die. But suicides rarely go more than a few hundred feet into the woods. A forest ranger told me that people who go into the forest to die "are always right where you can find them. And they don't set up camp."

I roamed aimlessly, trying to make tracks that would be found if anyone looked. But there was a big part of me that didn't want anyone to come searching—didn't want anyone else to get lost, didn't want anyone to know I was lost. And then, as I spun around, scanning for something familiar, I saw a faint glint of light, literally like a star through the woods. Was it a mirage? I couldn't tell. It was like a spaghetti strap to a drowning man. But it didn't make any difference; light meant warmth and shelter, and that's where I was headed. The anxiety drained from me as I trudged toward the light and soon I realized that it was my house, my family was home, the motion-detector spotlights tripped, and I was safe and sound. Them, too.

As I lay in bed that night I heard helicopters overhead. Bad night for a helicopter ride, I thought—subzero temperatures, seventy-mile-an-hour winds, and a dark, starless, moonless sky. I learned why in the next morning's paper: lost hikers on Mount Lafayette. Two men, Laurence Frederickson, fifty-five, and James Osborne, thirty-six. Frederickson had winter hiking experience, and he was dead. Osborne was found nearby, barely alive, his body temperature more than twenty degrees below normal.

They'd gone out for a winter hike up the Falling Waters Trail to the top of Little Haystack and across Razor Ridge to Mount Lincoln and Mount Lafayette. Somewhere along the way, the weather turned them back. Eventually, they became ice-encrusted by the frozen fog and rime ice, which sticks to you like tiny ice balls made of Velcro. They never made it down below the tree line, out of the wind and cold. The first night they hunkered down on the lee side of a rock, but the next day they were too spent to get themselves off the mountain. And unfortunately, since they were both bachelors, they were gone a full day before anyone knew to go looking.

Frederickson, known as Fred, was a driver for Concord Trailways. I'd been on his bus to South Station and Logan Airport in Boston. He was very friendly, an outdoorsman who told great stories about hiking and long-distance bike riding. But despite his experience and ability, the mountain took its due. The chest-deep snow on the ridge was impassable. Post-holing and wading through five-foot snow drifts while wearing a pack and bearing down on seventy-mile-an-hour winds will tire a marathon runner in just a few hundred yards.

Expert knowledge and all the best gear are no guarantee for success, or even survival. In the 1980s, the Army Special Forces did winter training on Mount Lafayette and one of the men died of exposure. Nick Howe, my former neighbor when I lived atop Mount Cleveland, has cataloged "150 years of misadventure in the Presidential Range" in his book, *Not Without Peril.* It's a dangerous place.

People hike and climb to test themselves, not the elements. We're there to face nature, not to tame it. The allure of rarefied beauty and solitude, to be someplace most people couldn't or wouldn't go, especially on the mountain that brought Frost to Franconia, is a temptation that we don't give in to lightly. Yet, mistakes happen, the unforeseen makes itself known at the worst possible moment, and sometimes the consequences are dire. Nearly every year someone dies in the Presidential Range, and that's likely never to change.

Not a week had passed since the most recent death on Lafayette, when a hiker from Boston text-messaged his girlfriend saying he was on Mount Lafayette, hopelessly lost, and needed a rescue. After that, the guy's relatives started leaving messages telling him to call 911 to activate the GPS beacon on his cell phone. All new cell phones have them; you can even set them so you can be found without calling 911. Which I don't recommend for everyday use, but on a dangerous winter hiking trip, alone of all things, it would have been a good idea. So once again—it was their third rescue from Lafayette in less than two months—the search-and-rescue teams, including the Huey chopper crew, braved the wind and snow (but not without flying once around my property a hundred feet off the treetops, looking at all the weird structures—we get a lot of small aircraft activity in the skies above our place, from the Franconia Airport, but I believe this is the first time we diverted a rescue mission), and five hours later, by a dangling cable, plucked him from the peak of the mountain in the dark of night. A good story to tell his grandchildren.

The very next day, two very experienced hikers and climbers, both firefighters and paramedics, fresh from a recent ice-climbing expedition in Colorado, Alex Obert and Steven McCay, prime candidates for Adrenaline Anonymous, undertook the ambitious task of hiking the entire Presidential Traverse, the eight highest peaks in the Northeast—in a single day. Doable, I suppose, but not by me anymore.

They began at the foot of Mount Madison at two thirty on Sunday morning. Their wheel man, Will Kirk, hiked the first peak with them and then headed down. He was driving the car to the other end of the range to the foot of Mount Washington, where he'd meet them at the Appalachian Mountain Club's new and opulent digs, the Highland Center. Or, as I like to call it, the Log Mahal.

When his buddies never showed up, at two thirty Monday morning he sounded the alarm. Immediately, thirty search-and-rescue workers—some of them Fish and Game officers, most of them volunteers—were alerted and assigned their search areas. Off they went to look, as they already had twice in the past week or so, and even with a helicopter it took them two days to find them.

The lost hikers spent their first night on Mount Eisenhower, which must have been as comforting as the man himself because it was an uneventful bivouac. They stayed warm and dry through the night. They knew that people were looking for them, and at the time, that probably seemed like a bigger deal than finding their way out. They're pros; they knew what a full-scale search-and-rescue operation entailed.

Unlike the first two rescues, they weren't tripped up by a blizzard—quite the opposite. It was an uncharacteristically warm day—it hit fifty degrees up on the mountain, which is fifty degrees warmer than it was supposed to be that time of year. And then it rained and the thick clouds made their GPS device inoperable. As soon as the temperature got above freezing, the snow pack began to melt, swelling the streams that Obert and McCay ought to have been able to skip across, making them impassable. They couldn't go any higher, and they couldn't get back down, either. So they wandered around for another day and landed in the Dry River Wilderness, an inhospitable place, a sort of *Bonfire of the Vanities* neighborhood for the mountain-climbing scene. If you get lost around Mount Washington, and you keep the wind at your back, Dry River is where you'll eventually find yourself. And you won't like it.

That night was less convivial than the one before and had them on their feet, sleepless, stamping themselves warm until the sun came up. The next day their tracks were spotted by the helicopter and quickly they were whooshed to safety and into the waiting arms of their families, who had been worried to death about them. As well they should.

In mid-May, as the last wisps of snow were melting from the mountain, the robins were pulling worms out of the ground, and I was finishing this book, a tourist from Shanghai, China, a young woman in her twenties, was climbing Mount Lafayette on this glorious spring day when a boulder up the path gave way and tumbled down the mountain, striking her and killing her instantly.

The White Mountains are an extreme playground. The jewel, Mount Washington, holds the record for the worst weather on the planet, set back in 1934 when an unexpected April storm kicked up 231-mile-an-hour winds—a good day not to be in the woods. It's important to remember that this is the same forest loggers work in, often alone, all their lives. Not for fun, or kicks, or aesthetics—for a job. It's a constant reminder that every living thing's time comes. Robert Frost understood. He said, "The figure for a whole life is a tree." Loggers get that better than anyone.

5

CLIMATE CHANGE
AND THE FOREST

The Long, Short, Warm,
Cold Winter of Our Discontent

The Bermuda Triangle got tired of warm
weather. It moved to Alaska. Now Santa
Claus is missing.
   Steven Wright

 I knew spring was here because my post office
box was stuffed with seed catalogs and the mud at
the end of our horse's paddock was a boot-sucking
knee deep. Mud season is a part of life in the northern woods.
This year was especially bad because of the lack of snow cover

throughout the winter. The ground didn't freeze so you couldn't drive a skidder over it until January nineteenth, and it was mud again by March twenty-second. Without the snow's insulating effect, the frost line was deeper, so when the thaw came, the mud was like Tarzan quicksand.

I pore over the seed catalogs looking for exotic varieties to make gardening a little more interesting, and like every backyard gardener, I'm restricted to the plants that will thrive in the climate zone I live in, which—for the moment—is Zone 4. Until relatively recently, that information was a constant, like my Social Security number. I figured if I learned it once, I'd know it forever.

But according to the National Oceanic and Atmospheric Administration, the winter of 2006–07 was the warmest on record worldwide. The combined land and ocean temperatures for December through February were 1.3 degrees Fahrenheit above average for the 127 years that records have been kept, and 11 of the last 12 years rank among the warmest since 1850, when global temperatures were first charted and logged. A century from now, Granite Staters could be buying seeds for Zones 6 through 9 and living in a climate like North Carolina's. And while the prospect of pruning a flowering hibiscus in my shirtsleeves in February might be appealing on some level, it poses an uncertain future for the region's forest economy.

Signs of climate change are everywhere—from drowning polar bears in the Arctic to drunken trees in Greenland, to sweeping desertification across China and Africa, and to no snow in the Alps for World Cup skiing. Noticeable changes are occurring much closer to home, too. Ice coverage on Lake Winnipesaukee has decreased by two full weeks in the last one hundred years. Loggers were shut out of the woods for nearly a month of unseasonable mud this winter. I should mention here that there are loggers, like Logger Bob, who think climate change is a plot dreamed up by the Bilderbergers to foist an untold number of new nuclear power plants on us. "The country's headed to Mad Max," Bob says at least a half-dozen times a day, ". . . and I'm ready for it."

Nonetheless, the effects of climate change are obvious, and the forest products and agricultural industries are hit more directly than most. According to a recent study by Innovative Natural Resource Solutions of Portland, Maine, at the current warming rate, in twenty-five years mud season could increase from twenty days to twenty-five days; in fifty years it could be as high as fifty days, and in one hundred years it will be eighty full days that loggers are out of the woods. Considering Logger Bob's claim that he'll be lucky to get three, maybe four full months in the woods this year, these seem like optimistic projections. Between 2004 and 2008, Bob's income was cut by more than half—some of this was due to the real estate market collapse, but it's primarily the result of the truncated logging season.

The cumulative loss to New Hampshire landowners due to a sixty-day increase in mud season over the next century is estimated at $11.5 billion, which translates as a $33.9 billion overall loss to the New Hampshire economy, and a $1.1 billion loss in timber yield taxes to New Hampshire towns and cities. Because the effects vary from region to region, a national loss figure would be pure speculation, but it's not unreasonable to presume a national shortfall in the hundreds of billions.

As the Northeast's climate gets warmer, the growing season will be longer, and the trees will grow faster. But as John Aber, vice president for research at the University of New Hampshire, points out, "A longer growing season means more water use, which could mean 20 to 30 percent less water flow in the streams, resulting in a diminished surface water supply." Moreover, it will create a "high robust factor" for fire. As the growing season is extended, so is the likelihood for drought and forest fires. Does New Hampshire have the wherewithal to cope with large-scale forest fires? Does anywhere in the Northeast? No. Our technical abilities haven't kept pace with reforestation. We haven't had a major fire since the nineteenth century—and those were due to the treetops and slash left behind by giant clear cuts that were ignited by the sparks from the old coal-burning trains.

"These woods are too wet to burn," Bob says. "We're not in any danger of that." I defer to his superior knowledge of most things woods-related, but the scientific community disagrees.

A study released in January 2008 by the Union of Concerned Scientists estimates that rising temperatures in the Northeast over the next fifty years—depending upon how we respond to the current situation—will range from three to eleven degrees Fahrenheit. But that's a twelve-month average. The seasonal breakdown means that in the winter it will be slightly warmer, and we won't get enough snow to insulate our native species from the frost. In the summer we could have sixty-six days over ninety degrees, compared to ten days now, and twenty-three days over one hundred degrees, compared to one day now—leading to a greater likelihood of interseason drought. By 2108,

Franconia could feel like Phoenix, Arizona, for much of the summer. Phoenix will be as dry and lifeless as a piece of old parchment.

Under these conditions, the red pine, balsam, red spruce, quaking aspen, paper and yellow birch, pin cherry, and larch will no longer be able to germinate. Drought-sensitive species, such as white ash and sugar maple, will suffer dieback. Warmer-climate trees—hickory, post oak, sweet gum, sourwood, and loblolly pine—will likely move into the forest, albeit slowly. The more cosmopolitan species with wind-dispersed seeds, such as the red oak and the aspen, will spread and reproduce the quickest.

John Aber suggests that we plant outlying populations of southern oak or southern pine now; that way, if climate change unfolds as predicted, future loggers can harvest a healthy stock of loblolly, rather than search for the dwindling supply of white pines.

As Professor Steve Hamburg of Brown University's Center for Environmental Studies points out, "It's not just climate change—it's air pollution, exotic pests, beech bark disease, woolly adelgid—these are the stresses our forests face." And none of them is going away anytime soon.

The process now under way will take a century and, according to Hamburg, "The switch will not be pretty." As the older species expire, the detritus will create a tinder box in the woods. The species available for logging will be very limited until reforestation is complete, and the culture of logging could very likely be one of the early casualties.

To explore that future and address how we might avoid it, I attended a conference on climate change and the northern forest

in March 2007, cosponsored by the Society for the Protection of
New Hampshire Forests, and Clean Air, Cool Planet. The or-
ganizers expected about 100 people—350 showed up. Leading
researchers, foresters, loggers, conservationists, timberland owners, and just plain folks who know the woods and have seen
the changes attended the one-day affair. The scientists in
attendance—practitioners who have been studying global warming for twenty years—were delighted by the turnout. As one
panelist remarked, six months ago you could have held the same
confab inside a Toyota Prius.

Professional foresters, climate modelers, biologists, and
economists drove home the same overarching point: the environment is a closed system dictated by cause and effect, and the consequences of unchecked climate change will have long-lasting
economic and biological impacts on our forests and the forest-
products industry.

Tree and bush species are dying, and perhaps less-desirable,
warmer-climate species could move in sooner than later. According to Eric Kingsley, vice president of Innovative Natural Resource Solutions, hotter summers, longer mud seasons, and less
snow may have already sealed the fate of the sugar maple in New
Hampshire. Air pollution, acid rain, and the simple fact that
many people favor sugar maples where they shouldn't be planted
also contribute to the possible demise of the species. Kingsley's
research indicates that if conditions don't change drastically and
rapidly, in fifty years the maple syrup industry in New Hampshire may be nothing but a sweet memory. His worst-case scenario says maple sugaring in New Hampshire, Vermont, and
Maine could be effectively moribund by the end of this decade.

Phil Bryce, New Hampshire state forester, stacked climate change's effects on New Hampshire's forests in three tiers: direct threats, opportunities, and unintended consequences. For those who have seen Al Gore's film *An Inconvenient Truth* (and for most who haven't), direct threats are what come to mind first— intense and devastating weather events. Torrential rains (New Hampshire has had three one-hundred-year floods in the last three years), killing ice storms (two in the last two years), droughts (two in the last three years), and high winds (a hurricane at my house in the White Mountains in April 2007 sustained eighty- to ninety-mile-an-hour winds, tearing up trees as tall as four-story buildings)—these will all seriously undermine the forest's health. Changes in the climate will also make native tree species more susceptible to insect infestation and disease. These are especially problematic variables due to their unpredictability—pests will come, but we don't know when or which ones; ice storms will happen, but not on schedule.

Uncertainty is heightened by the closed-loop nature of the environment, making it difficult to determine the rapidity at which noticeable environmental shifts might occur. One variable tends to exacerbate another, turning incremental change into exponential devastation.

For instance, do more-intense rainstorms mean the culverts required for logging roads are too small? Are the bridges and pole fords loggers build over streams adequate to mitigate silt and sediment from migrating into habitats and drinking-water reservoirs? Because if we don't address these issues, and there are fewer trees growing to absorb the nitrogen in the soil, it will wash away and find its way into drinking water in the form of nitrates. High nitrate levels in water can result in methemoglo-binemia, or "blue baby syndrome."

It works this way: the nitrates convert to nitrite, which is absorbed into the blood and hemoglobin. The nitrite then con-verts the body's hemoglobin to methemoglobin. Hemoglobin carries the oxygen in the blood, but methemoglobin is much less efficient at this—resulting in a lower oxygen supply to our vital organs: the heart, the lungs, the brain. Adults' bodies are fairly adept at reconverting methemoglobin to hemoglobin, but in-fants are not, and severe methemoglobinemia can cause brain damage and even death. Consider that cycle of life—dead trees equals dead babies.

Prolonged exposure to high levels of nitrates is linked to gastric problems and has been shown to cause cancer in test ani-mals. As much as we'd like to think of ourselves as in control of our environment, in the end we're only a part of it. And in the case of anthropogenic CO_2, we are a negative actor on the scene. We sow what we reap.

Fortunately, unless you're completely change-averse, it's not all bad news. For the foreseeable future, a different forest and cli-mate are unavoidable, but it doesn't necessarily have to follow the worst-case scenario. Getting beyond the unknown and em-bracing the inevitable are, for the short-term, the only ways to comfortably survive what's coming.

Vibrant markets for low-grade wood are essential to the practice of sustainable forestry—mainly because a lot of junk trees grow in the northern forest. Balsams and other softwoods that never get big enough to be saw logs for the mill populate the forest in huge numbers. Until the last decade, mills in northern

New Hampshire produced millions of tons of brown paper bags, toilet paper, copy paper, and newsprint. But much of that business has moved west to the giant tree farms where they grow weed trees genetically tweaked to mature quickly. A large portion of the market is also filled by foreign markets—countries in eastern Europe, South and Central America, and the Pacific rim, where environmental standards are lax, and clear cutting is the norm.

North of Berlin, New Hampshire, where the forest once seemed endlessly bountiful, some of it's been all but picked clean of low-grade wood. Not entirely, but it isn't the wood-chip resource it once was, and will be again someday, Mother Nature permitting. The loss of market share and dwindling stock leaves the guys with logging equipment to pay off, mortgages to meet, and families to feed in some serious, long-term difficulty.

Enter the use of forest biomass for wood energy. The former wood-pulp plant in Berlin, New Hampshire, is slated to become a 50-megawatt electricity-generating plant, which will create an opportunity to offset the loss of traditional markets in the pulp and paper industry. New Hampshire currently has six wood-fired electricity-generating plants producing 118 megawatts of electricity; another 50-megawatt plant is planned. The Schiller Station in Newington, New Hampshire, eats 130 tractor-trailers—nearly four thousand tons—of wood chips every day.

Wood's energy potential doesn't end with electricity. Cellulosic ethanol—fuel made from low-grade wood chips—is cleaner-burning and thirteen times more efficient than corn-based ethanol. When it becomes commercially available sometime in the next decade (a Massachusetts company, Mascoma

Corporation, a $100 million company, has the inside track on developing a process that uses enzymes, organisms to break down and convert feedstock such as wood chips and switch grass into ethanol), it could easily fill in the market gaps left by the changing pulp and paper industry.

Biofuels made from corn, sugar, and palm oil are driving up the cost of food worldwide. With 30 percent of all corn grown in the United States going to ethanol production, the price of milk and beef are skyrocketing. In 2000, worldwide production of ethanol was roughly five billion gallons; in 2008, it's estimated that fifteen billion gallons will be produced in the United States alone.

In developing countries, the demand for biofuels is creating a new wave of cash-crop-economy woes. The amount of corn required to produce a single tank of ethanol—twenty gallons— could feed a person on a two-thousand-calorie-per-day diet for a year. But the problem goes beyond a corn shortage.

According to Oxfam, the London-based antihunger charity, with all the best arable land dedicated to growing biofuel crops, small farmers all over the developing world are left with hillsides and sandpits in which to grow rice and beans. The same problem arose in the twentieth century with coffee, cotton, sugar, and bananas. In order to artificially suppress the prices of these crops to make them household staples in developed economies, peasant farmers were pushed off their land and left with little opportunity to provide sustenance for their families—because if you feed people coffee, cotton, sugar, and bananas, to the exclusion of everything else, they're not going to grow up big and strong, if at all. Biofuel demand, especially in Europe and increasingly in the

United States, is creating another lopsided international agricultural policy that fulfills the desires of the developed world while ignoring the needs of developing nations.

Even the World Bank and International Monetary Fund—the lending agencies that, as conditions for providing loans, required the agricultural policies that led to the cash crop/food crop imbalance—agree that the production of biofuels is having the unintended consequence of food shortages and breadline riots around the world. When the price of rice spiked by 75 percent between February and April 2008, the World Bank issued a warning to the developed world that the food riots in Indonesia, the Philippines, Cameroon, Egypt, and Haiti—where five people were killed and the prime minister was ousted—are just the beginning. According to World Bank president Robert Zoellick, the lives of 100 million people are threatened by deeper poverty and possible starvation.

Cellulosic ethanol would be an elegant fix to the problem—nobody eats trees anyway, and they pretty much grow wild. Of course, it requires a managed and sustainable approach, but since trees are North America's largest crop, it certainly bears watching as a replacement for other ethanol sources.

In fact, Laurie Wayburn, president of the Pacific Forest Trust, in California, believes the United States could become "the Middle East of Wood Chips"—a large-scale energy exporter to Europe, where they have far more wood-to-energy plants than we do, but far fewer trees.

Cutting trees isn't Wayburn's game; quite the opposite. She's a pioneer in using the forest to offset industrial carbon output in California, and sees America's forest as its richest natural resource. Wayburn is a big believer in saving trees, but she also sees the need for working forests as an alternative to fossil fuels.

Sequestration isn't a new policy—land trusts have been buying development easements on large tracts of real estate for more than a hundred years. Think of what Wayburn does as an energy easement. Current-use real estate tax laws do essentially the same thing. On our property, we have eighteen of twenty-two acres in current use, which means they're wooded, undeveloped, and will remain that way. For this concession, I'm taxed one-third of what I'm taxed on the four cleared acres that surround our house. In my mind, those eighteen acres in current use are carbon-sequestered, and for that, I get to drive a Ford F-150 pickup—but only to plow my driveway and go to the dump.

Wide-ranging research shows that the forest is nature's most effective means of encapsulating CO_2 and mitigating the ravages of climate change. Forest sequestration can significantly reduce greenhouse-gas emissions in three ways: the sustainable management of existing timber lots; slowing the rate of deforestation; and increasing the overall carbon sink with the establishment of new forests. It also tends to reduce forest fragmentation, which is a boon to wildlife.

Let's take them one at a time. The planet's forests are its largest and most efficient tool to mitigate global warming. Trees, in case you—as I did—slept through botany, breathe CO_2 in, and oxygen out. Which is mainly why flora and fauna get along so well together. The CO_2 that a tree respires remains within that tree, until it falls over and expires. As it rots, it exudes the CO_2 it contained. It can also give off its CO_2 when someone cuts it down and feeds it into a woodstove, or a biomass electricity plant. But that's still CO_2 neutral, because it came from the current cycle. Hydrocarbons—oil, coal, and gas—emit CO_2 that came from the Flintstones. The earth is a self-regulating mechanism, and over the past 150 years we've pumped a whaleload of CO_2 into our atmosphere—that's the thin bubble we live in—that was retired with the dinosaurs.

This is why wood-generated electricity plants are carbon neutral, while oil- and coal-fired plants are not. The CO_2 in the wood chips would be expired whenever that tree died; releasing its carbon dioxide faster by burning it doesn't contribute to its overall effect because another tree will grow in its place. That's how a well-managed forest works. Oil and coal, however, have sequestered ancient carbon for aeons and in a hundred short years we've let it all loose on the world again.

New Hampshire's "25 by 25" policy is geared to shift at least 25 percent of the state's energy use to alternative sources by 2025, and will undoubtedly increase the demand for wood chips to burn and generate electricity. Will that revive the logging industry? Not according to Mike Geyer: "Chipping is not logging. A chip is a chip, a log is a log, and they have very different uses." Which is true, because most of the trees involved in what Mike considers logging go into building products—from framing to cabinetry. And one of the best ways to encapsulate CO_2 in a tree is to build a house out of it, and take good care of it.

"Where's the romance in a machine scooping up five trees at a time and feeding them into a giant chipper?" Mike asked. "Why would I come into the woods every morning to do that?"

New technologies—such as wood products and processes

for reducing wood fiber to its hydrocarbon components, and then reworking it to replace petroleum-based plastics—are now being developed. In many ways, the forest remains an untapped resource, its potential waiting to be unleashed by innovations born of necessity. Increased capital investment and government incentives could bring these and other new uses for wood to market much quicker. It's a vast natural resource that the government supports very little—when compared to other agricultural subsidies, independent logging doesn't exist. And if conditions don't improve soon, independent loggers won't, either.

All the way over on the other side of the country, forest sequestration is a growing part of the mix in California's carbon market; it's a workable program anywhere there are large forests, or where they can be created, such as on dormant agricultural land or otherwise useless real estate, and then left alone forever. Or at least until the temperature starts to drop.

There's money in it. If you've got forestland in California to sequester, you can earn carbon credits with it. You can put your resource in Humboldt County to work absorbing the CO_2 from some smokestack operation down in Los Angeles that burns tanker-loads of hydrocarbons. You either have to install a prohibitively expensive pollution-control system that will solve the problem, or buy your forest's carbon credits and call it a wash. So, sequestration isn't exactly a solution—it's mitigation until we can figure out what we're going to do to really fix the problem. And Laurie Wayburn knows that a big part of the answer lies in the potential of working forests.

Sequestration's benefits are more variable in the Northeast—and therefore less viable—than in climates with less seasonal fluctuation. Trees in this part of the country are on about 120 days per year. After that, you get no work out of them. They just stand there. On the other hand, the northern forest is young and still sucking up plenty of CO_2. The old-growth forests in California aren't growing anymore, not drinking up much carbon dioxide. They're maintaining. As John Aber put it, "I'm not so sure they're not counting twice." While the old-growth forests are encapsulating a whole lot of CO_2, they're less effective as carbon sinks; they're not huffing the stuff like a growing and vibrant forest does.

In New Hampshire, 80 percent of the forestland is in private hands—many of them ten- and twenty-acre-woodlot owners. This presents the typical sequestration scheme, which usually means contracting vast tracts of land with a single negotiation and contract, with a new and very wily set of details to manage. But not, perhaps, deal killers. As Laurie Wayburn points out, the Pacific Forest Trust was modeled after the Society for the Protection of New Hampshire Forests.

All that said, the potential unintended consequences of forest sequestration aren't trivial. We can only speculate on the demands it might put on land-use policy. Will agricultural and grazing land be afforested to take advantage of carbon credits? Will development have to compete financially with nondevelopment? And since California's experience proves that sequestration can be more profitable than logging, could it supplant the forest-products industry as timber's highest and best use?

Every option taken or passed over will have its own set of outcomes. For instance, how will we ensure that the growing demand for wood chips won't result in unsustainable forestry practices? A truckload of chips is the same whether it comes from a wide swath of saplings (pecker poles) or a dense thicket of balsam ready to be harvested. Once it's chips, who's to say where it came from?

If we simply allow the maples (currently selling at more than six hundred dollars per thousand board feet) to be replaced by a less valuable species, will logging become patently unprofitable, or will the market change in concert with the forest?

The forest needs a seat at the table when public policy decisions affecting climate change are made. Mandates and incentives will drive the issue in the years to come, and if the forest-products industry, timber-lot owners, and conservationists don't fully participate, the outcome may not protect their interests.

The predictions are dire, but there's reason to be hopeful. Options are available that can halt and eventually roll back many of the effects of global warming. With the right mix of official policies and personal choices, we can fix the environment and save the forest.

Bob has other ideas. "You want to know how to control the weather?" he asked me. "I have a method, works every time. If I go out and get good and drunk tonight, no matter what the weatherman says, it won't rain tomorrow because I'll have to get up early with a pounding squash and go to work in the woods."

6

THE FOREST CIRCUS

Mr. Ranger isn't going to like this, Yogi.
Boo Boo Bear

 Land ownership in the East has dictated the type of logging we do. In New Hampshire, logging is a 350-year-old industry—think about it, the first thing on the pilgrims' to-do list, before they could build shelter or grow food, was to log the land. Today, 84 percent of New Hampshire land is privately owned, most of it in woodlots of twenty-five acres or less. That fragmentation makes large, mechanized logging operations overkill by an order of magnitude, like mowing your grass with a corn combine. Most logging here is done by the hundreds of lone Brush Cats. It's a demonstrably good system because, after three and a half centuries of logging, New Hampshire's number-one industry is tourism—which suggests that we've struck a healthy balance between commerce and beauty.

But we work hard at it. In 1901 the Society for the Protection of the New Hampshire Forests was founded. That was four years before Teddy Roosevelt launched the U.S. Forest Service. We take our trees seriously—we appreciate them, we use them, and we care for them. At least we try to. In 1908, seven years before the National Park Service was founded, the society convinced the New Hampshire state legislature to purchase Crawford's Notch—named for Abel and Ethan Crawford, who helped settle this part of the world and built the country's first hiking trails in and around the notch. From Hart's Location down into Twin Mountain, up and around Mount Washington, which is very nearly the highest peak in the East—Mount Mitchell in North Carolina is 396 feet higher, but we don't talk about it— the Crawfords invented recreational hiking. Before that, it was jut walking in the mountains to get somewhere.

Forty years ago, a bit farther south, down in the foothills of the White Mountains, Robert Marcalus and some partners bought a 6,578-acre piece of forest known as Green Acre Woodlands, which spreads across the Cardigan highlands through the towns of Groton, Hebron, Rumney, Dorchester, and Plymouth, New Hampshire. Today, 96 percent of that land is working forest, producing a half million board feet a year—pulp wood, saw logs, and wood chips for the bioenergy market. It's a well-run woodlot that contributes to the local economy, provides an alternative energy source, and supports wildlife. But all that could change.

Green Acres is New Hampshire's largest single parcel of land south of the White Mountains and for that reason is significant to conservationists. It's an important living space for bears, moose, raptors, fishers, coyotes, and songbirds—species that require plenty of breathing room and roaming space. It has miles of frontage and riparian habitat along the Baker River, Halls Brook, Wise Brook, and Groton Hollow Brook, as well as miles of hiking and snowmobile trails, sweeping views, rolling hills, flats, and overlooks.

In addition to creating a wildlife habitat in what had been an afforested agricultural field, Green Acres' timber managers have given a wide berth to a ghost town. Up at the top of the first pitch in the property, overlooking the Cardigan highlands, a former farming village—nobody knows its name—has lain undisturbed for more than 160 years. Its stone-lined well remains intact; the foundation for the tavern dominates the landscape and is surrounded by a dozen or so cellar holes where houses once stood, where the families who farmed this part of New Hampshire once lived. The last resident left this village in 1840, meaning that more than two decades before the Civil War, this little community was already a memory.

I sat in the middle of that ghost town and tried to imagine life in northern New Hampshire when it was settled. Hilly, rocky soil, five-month-long winters, black flies as thick as storm clouds, and Abenaki Indians with attitude. *Abenaki* means "Real People," and the name they gave this place, *Ndakinna*, means "Our Land." So, putting down roots here was frowned upon. Yet, these settlers did, and it struck me, as I hopped over the open well for the eighth or ninth time, that the overwhelming desire to pioneer that drew people to places like this exists today only in derivative applications for the Internet and episodes of MTV's *Jackass*. The "pioneer spirit" may be a cliché, and pure nostalgia in the age of McWorld, but that's because drinking the water in Cancún and having unprotected sex are as close as most Americans ever get to the edge of the abyss anymore.

The New England countryside is littered with these bygone little burgs. A few miles from my house there's an old village called Bungay; its physical remnants are long gone and the place now exists only in our oral history, but that's enough. Bungay, they say, was an enclave of Puritans who rejected Cotton Mather as a liberal wussy tool of Satan. They were, apparently, the Puritan SS, and I'm positive there are still a few around. If not, then Bungay's only real legacy is the Bungay Jar. "Jar" is logger talk for a seasonal and forceful wind, presumably because it will *jar* a man off his feet, or a tree out of the ground. Or maybe because it blows so hard that you feel like you're caught in a jar with it. No one seems to know. Bob thinks it's all crap. "The wind doesn't blow any worse here than anywhere else," he says. "The Bungay Jar is just an excuse for shitty workmanship by Yankee farmers too cheap to use enough damn nails when they build something." That's a minority opinion, but duly noted.

The Bungay Jar originates down at the end of Route 116, at the base of Mount Moosilauke, and it bellows through the Easton Valley clear over to Mount Agassiz—which is named for Louis Agassiz, one of the most eminent naturalists of the nineteenth century, a scientific polymath whose true passion was scientific racism, which posited that people could be cataloged climatically, as if we were plants. It was, in essence, an anti-Darwin protoapartheid that he peddled from a tenured chair at Harvard. But that was a different time, as we say, so it didn't stop people from naming lakes and mountains for him all over the world, or

Henry Wadsworth Longfellow from writing a poem about him. In 2007, the Swiss government acknowledged Agassiz's unvarnished racism, but they voted to keep the Agassizhorn intact nonetheless. As we keep Mount Agassiz.

In the early 1990s, I lived on the windward side of Mount Agassiz, atop Mount Cleveland, named for our first environmental president, Grover, whose great-grand-nephew lives over around Conway and is available to address your annual meeting or company Christmas party as his famous forebear, in character and full period dress. One night, the Bungay Jar came roaring up the valley and slammed into our cabin so fiercely that it picked it up off its phone-pole pilings and dropped it so abruptly that it cracked the picture window and broke my favorite coffee mug. It's a good thing we didn't really own anything, because it could have been much worse. Newton's first law says that bodies in motion tend to stay in motion, and we were definitely moving. Another gust right behind that one would have rolled our two-story, twenty-by-twenty cabin on its roof like a turtle in the dirt.

The roof was the problem—the house faced the wind and the roof had a huge overhang. It looked a little like a cedar-shaked stealth bomber. Our outhouse, which was rotated ninety degrees from the house and presented its pitched side to the Bungay Jar, stood unmolested. Not a centimeter of movement—thank God— while the house nearly got tossed down the mountain.

Loggers get driven out of the woods by the wind all the time. To be in the forest in a big blow, with trees cracking all around you, the sway and the snap of one-hundred-foot pines and the deafening roar—you can run, but not fast enough. It's a nightmare.

All that said, aside from the wind and the interminable winters, for real estate developers, the White Mountains and their foothills smell like my composter to black bears—as far as they're concerned, it's theirs for the taking. Robert Marcalus's six-thousand-plus acres are just such a piece of land: ripe for development, particularly for housing lots designated as "majestic," which is to say big and beautiful. The market for million-dollar second homes in New Hampshire has boomed in the twenty-first century—everybody from Whoopi Goldberg to Mitt Romney has a place here. In the past five years, trophy houses have sprouted in my town like mushrooms in the spring—and I seldom see anyone in them.

These majestic lots are purely for the economic elite and, as extravagant possessions go, they're big baubles, not homesteads. These developments create, in essence, villages that are abandoned before anyone ever really lives in them.

The trade-off is a bad deal not just for loggers and the wood industry but for the communities. If a developer turns a five-thousand-acre tract into fifty hundred-acre sites, the wood to build those fifty homes represents what a well-run, sustainable logging operation would take off that land in less than a year. In return, the community gets more houses on its tax rolls and a few short-term construction jobs. What it loses is land that was once productive, providing jobs and recreation for generations, clean water, and healthy wildlife. Once the land passes from forestland to subdivision, all that is either lost or shuttered to the public forever.

Robert Marcalus very much wants to maintain Green Acres as a working forest, to keep the loggers and the mills in business and the countryside accessible to the public. But land always changes hands eventually—deals change, people die, taxes become unaffordable. The only way to protect the forest long-term is through conservation and development easements.

Over the past decade, with funding from the U.S. Forest Service's Forest Legacy Program, the New Hampshire Division of Forest and Lands has secured development easements on 208,807 acres of working forests—preserving timberlands, reducing the fragmentation of wildlife habitats, and either creating or maintaining public access for outdoor recreation. All New Hampshire FLP conservation easements restrict development and require sustainable forestry practices and public access. The land remains in private hands, but it can't be developed—a sort of free-market socialism, which is a hybrid that the United States government has used in other economic sectors for sixty years.

Phil Bryce, director of the New Hampshire Division of Forest and Lands, regards the FLP as essential to the future of New Hampshire's forests: "The FLP does very well in capturing the benefits of the forest's complexity. It accommodates logging, manufacturing, tourism, and recreation, which combined have a $475-per-acre annual value to the state economy. With biomass energy demands likely to triple in the near future, the preservation of the state's working forests will only become more important to the state's livelihood."

Put simply, the FLP is a voluntary program providing federal funds to assist states in land acquisition and the acquisition of development rights on privately owned, select parcels of forestlands. The U.S. Forest Service funds up to 75 percent of project costs, with the balance coming from private, state, or local sources.

New Hampshire's first FLP project, completed in 1996, is known as the Jahoda and Jahoda/Johnson parcel—two tracts in Pittsburg's "big empty." But, according to Paul Doscher, the New Hampshire Forest Society's vice president for Land Conservation, the FLP has its roots eight years earlier, in northern New Hampshire's forty-thousand-acre Nash Stream Forest project.

In 1988, the former Diamond International Paper land holdings in northern New Hampshire were owned by Claude Rancourt, who had plans to subdivide the property and develop portions of it. At the same time, the Northern Forest Lands Council suggested a new federal program that would allow the U.S. Forest Service to purchase conservation easements on private property; the Nash Stream project became the prototype. It was such a success that the U.S. Department of Agriculture created the FLP in 1992 and funded its first projects in 1993. In 1996, the U.S. Farm Bill changed the FLP in an important way—unlike earlier projects, the federal government still provides the funding, but now the states hold the easements. That single modification made the program far more attractive to private landowners reluctant to make the federal government any more a part of their lives than it already was. State government is a little less ominous because it's at least marginally more accountable to its citizens.

Now, the very tip of northern New Hampshire—170,000 acres—is privately owned and logged, but remains lush, beautiful, and publicly accessible for hunting, fishing, snowmobiling, four-wheeling, two-wheeling, hiking, bird-watching, or just lying in the grass looking at the darkest sky you'll find anywhere.

Since 1996, New Hampshire has used the FLP to protect more working forests than any other state in the nation except Maine. And when considered as a percentage of available forest-land, New Hampshire's participation well exceeds even Maine's. According to the USDA's Kathryn Conant, FLP national program manager, "The New Hampshire Forest Legacy Program is one of the oldest and most successful programs in the country, and has become a strong leader and model for other states."

Nationally, the FLP has grown from a $10 million program serving two states in 1993, to its current $66 million appropriation with thirty-seven states participating, and another nine ready to sign on. The federal budget for the next fiscal year cuts the FLP by 78 percent, to less than $15 million. The budget calls for similar cuts in other conservation and wildlife programs at USDA.

So, a wildly useful and successful federal program popular across the political spectrum, the immediate benefits of which will be measured in geologic time, can't catch a break in Washington. Seems like a good investment. But even at current funding, the federal government can manage to find only $66 million a year for it. The budgetary folly of the federal government is legend: it spends $66 million on coffeemakers and toilet seats and hammers, not to mention $45 cans of Coke in Iraq. According to Nobel Prize winner Joseph Stiglitz, the federal government spends $5,000 per second in Iraq. The Forest Legacy Program's budget currently equals the cost of one F-16 fighter jet, an infinitesimal amount of federal oil and agricultural subsidies, or .066 percent of a trillion dollars in tax breaks Washington gave to the top 1 percent of income earners in the country. It's not, by Washington standards, a lot of money, and one might think that a figure ten times that amount would be more appropriate. Yet, it's on the chopping block in Washington.

The FLP doesn't fund isolated development rights with no grander scheme in mind. Each parcel the FLP takes out of development is another piece in the puzzle that ensures public access to beautiful places, clean water, and the most efficient way to capture and sequester CO_2, the major culprit behind climate change. Yet, because of insufficient funding, Phase II of the Cardigan Highlands project will have to wait for the next round of funding—which may not exist—as will Kimball Hill, another twenty-seven hundred acres of forestland in the southwest corner of Groton and a key linkage in the north–south corridor of contiguous forest connecting the Cardigan Highlands and the Newfound Lake Watershed with the White Mountain National Forest.

The Kimball Hill property is a working forest of hardwoods, spruces, firs, sugar maples, beeches, and yellow birches, with an extensive system of snowmobile trails and hiking paths that could easily link to the Appalachian Trail. In another area, there's a pocket of likely old-growth forest on a hillside too steep to log, and a rock canyon resembling the famous Sculptured Rocks site in Groton.

What's more, the Green Acres and Kimball Hill properties anchor the northern end of the Quabbin to Cardigan Partnership, or Q2C—a two-state landscape-scale conservation plan that runs from the Quabbin Reservoir in Belchertown, Massachusetts, to Mount Cardigan in New Hampshire. Losing any one of these parcels to development will disrupt a natural flow of land and water that we can never get back.

So it's a good thing that the U.S. Forest Service has done, and we appreciate it. But hang around with loggers long enough and you'll get an earful about its less-than-constructive activity. The trend in the national forest is toward mechanized logging operations, mainly because the timber sales are of sufficient size to warrant it, but also because mechanized logging is twice as safe as chainsaw and skidder logging. Cutting the danger in half puts mechanized logging on a par with commercial fishing.

Bob, and others, regard the timber sales on national forestland to be a form of corporate socialism. "When you don't have to cut your own roads, you've reduced the cost and time of doing a job pretty significantly," Bob says. "And who has to compete with that subsidy? Me. All that federal wood glutting the market at a time when nobody's building nothing? Just cut my throat and get it over with."

Harvesting pulp wood for cogeneration biomass plants that produce electricity, or for cellulosic ethanol—which is far more efficient than corn- or sugar-based ethanols—may well replace the paper industry as the best use of New Hampshire's low-grade wood crop. As the North Country learned in the harshest way possible, there's a finite market for paper. But is the demand for electricity and fuel finite? It doesn't appear to be. In the past decade, all across the U.S. South and Southwest, summer heat waves have forced rolling brownouts—energy cuts caused by a lack of generating capacity. The grid wants more juice.

According to the USDA, a cogeneration wood plant consumes about one thousand acres per one hundred thousand tons of annual capacity. Public Service of New Hampshire, the state's largest public utility, opened its Schiller cogeneration plant in Newington in 2007—it eats five thousand acres of trees every year. I toured the plant the month it opened—watched a load of wood chip processed by a giant shaker system that separated the wheat from the chaff. I use a similar system for my compost, except this one runs up into the plant like a giant Rube Goldberg contraption, while mine is sixteen feet square, made from two-by-fours and chicken wire. But the concept is the same. The crème de la crème of the wood chips are separated from sticks and pine cones and pieces of barbed wire, then burned. The heat boils water, which produces steam, which turns the giant turbine, which generates electricity. It's essentially the same process that PSNH's nuclear plant uses thirteen miles down the coast, in Seabrook, except there are no spent fuel rods, no China Syndrome, no protesters, and a far more sustainable and renewable resource.

All the commercial biomass plants in the state combined take approximately twelve thousand acres annually. Three additional plants currently proposed will eat another fifteen thousand acres per year when they come online. At their height, the pulp mills in Berlin and Groveton ate about a million tons of chips apiece each year.

In Groveton, in 1984, the mill manager showed me the process by which they create "wood flour," in which trees are pulverized into dust, bleached, and rinsed. He asked me to guess their biggest client. I had no idea. It's cellulose, so it has no nutritional value to the human body. So I guessed the most obvious and said, "Building materials." "Nope," he said. "McDonald's." I'm sure I grimaced. I immediately started thinking french fries, hamburger filler . . . "Nondairy shakes," he said with a smirk. "What do you think the nondairy part is? Water, sugar, flavoring, and wood flour. That's your nondairy shake." He was right. I'd never given much thought to what that nondairy designation meant. But people don't understand dairy very well. I remember asking a clerk in the market in Groveton where the eggs were. "In the dairy department," she said with an edge in her young voice that implied I was an idiot for not knowing that cows laid eggs.

Because the mills used so many trees for so many things for so many years, some cite that as proof that there's ample pulpwood in the forest to sustain these operations indefinitely. Then there are others, loggers mostly, who say the northern end of New Hampshire has been picked nearly clean of low-grade wood. And on that point, I could not find consensus. The U.S. Forest Service, the Society for the Protection of New Hampshire Forests, and the New Hampshire Timberland Owners Association say the forest produces more trees every year than get cut. Still, the trees need time to grow—fifty years for some. Pulpwood needs twenty years of growth—even the genetically tricked-out trees grown on big corporate farms out west need a decade to mature. So there's a point at which timber harvesting could get ahead of the curve and begin to deplete the forest, as it did a hundred years ago.

This is where the U.S. Forest Service plays an official role. The move to revert currently roadless areas to logging indicates that other areas are, at least for the present, lacking in low-grade wood. There are hundreds of miles of roads in the national forest, and since current demand for pulp doesn't come close to what it was when the paper mills were running, it gives credence to the charge that the forest has been overforested.

It's not as if it can't happen. In Minnesota, logging has increased by 60 percent since 1980, and as I write this, many hundreds of acres are being clear cut. Environmentalists say that no matter how you dress it up, the rate of deforestation is unsustainable for wildlife and bad for the overall ecology. In just twenty-five years, the moose population there has dropped from 4,000 to 237, victims of a shrinking habitat and climate change.

Moose are rugged critters that like the cold, which is why you find them in the country's northernmost regions, usually in the mountains. In warmer areas, they're susceptible to parasites—ticks especially. Here in northern New Hampshire, the same sleek and handsome moose that terrorize my garden and chase my dog in spring are, by late summer, laden with big bloated ticks hanging off their undersides like the fringe on an overstuffed ottoman. The cold weather used to kill the ticks, but warmer temperatures are allowing winter ticks to survive. They literally suck the animal dry, and are becoming the leading cause of moose mortality—even more deadly than the five hundred hunters who win a moose tag in the lottery every year, and the flatlanders in their speeding SUVs.

Moose around here clearly get heat-stressed in ways I'd not seen before—and I see it all the time. Last summer, on a particularly hot and sticky July evening, I spied a moose and her two calves in my garden, laying waste to whatever looked edible. So

I went out with a pan in each hand, banging them together like a crazy man. They completely ignored me—I got the sense that they'd seen this tactic before, and besides, if all those ticks don't drive them out of their minds, a little noise isn't going to have much effect. So I got the hose and turned it on them. This wasn't very smart, because mama moose are like any other maternal mammal, except they're as big as draft horses and faster. When I hit her with a blast of water from the hose, her nostrils flared and she dropped her head as if to charge me. If she had, I'd have landed in a tree somewhere, but she didn't. She just looked at me with those big brown eyes, shimmied a little, then stood sideways so I could wet her down entirely. The calves immediately joined in the fun, playing in the spray, kicking and bucking, rolling through my arugula. All this was fine for the moose and for interspecies relations in general, but it wasn't helping my garden any. So when they were good and wet, I went inside, got my daughter's portable karaoke machine, and played a high-pitched feedback through the speaker, which sent them all scurrying into the woods.

New Hampshire's moose population stands at seven thousand, and, like Minnesota, without proper precautions, we could be down to a few hundred within a couple of decades. Warmer temperatures can't be helped in the short term, but the preservation of moose habitats can, and that's where good forestry and regulations come into play. When the woods can no longer sustain moose, we'll already be well on our way to the destruction of the forest.

To investigate the tree situation in northern New Hampshire, I went straight to the source and spent a morning with John

Harrigan up in Colebrook, New Hampshire. I've been going to Colebrook since I was a kid, back when I rode my motorcycle up and down the dirt roads, through the woods, and around the Connecticut Lakes. John's a native who lives on the lip of the Big Empty completely by choice. He was once offered the job of environmental reporter for the *Boston Globe,* but after driving around Boston for a day, he decided it wasn't for him.

He's an outdoor writer and hunter, and he comes by it all honestly. His father, Fred, a Harvard Law grad, bought the Colebook *News and Sentinel* just after World War II and raised a newspaper family. John's sister works at *Newsday,* in New York City, and his brother is an editor at the *Los Angeles Times.* In 2003, John's daughter and her husband took over the Colebrook *News and Sentinel.*

But John hasn't retired—when he isn't writing his many columns, he's in the woods looking for something to write about. We drove up to Pittsburg, New Hampshire together, tooling around in his truck, inspecting the forest for the trees, which he says are "healthy, sure, except there's no pine left up here."

John gets up at four thirty every morning, and often sees sixty-five-year-old loggers at five A.M., still bent and sore from the day before, heading into the woods just as the sun rises so they can get one extra load cut every day. "It's a tight business," John explains. "Tough, tough to make a living."

There's something odd about Colebrook—perhaps because of its proximity to Canada, or maybe because it's so far off the path—but through no fault of its own, the town attracts a bad element every now and then. The first culprit was Harry K. Thaw, scion of a Pittsburgh, Pennsylvania steel dynasty, a violent cokehead who was expelled from Harvard for chasing a taxi driver through the streets of Cambridge with a shotgun. A few years later, jealousy over his wife, Evelyn Nesbit, led Thaw to murder the architect Stanford White in a nightclub on the roof of the original Madison Square Garden. Some say he was enraged at learning that White had used his wife as a nude model for a statue at the Garden, a building that he designed and in which he lived in the penthouse. Others claim that White had warned Broadway's showgirls to stay away from the dangerous and crazy Thaw, which Harry found out about. In any case, White was dead and Thaw remanded to the Matteawan State Hospital for the Criminally Insane. He wandered off one day with a lot of outside help, but was put back in custody in Colebrook, New Hampshire, after being nabbed in Sherbrooke, Quebec. This incident is a storyline in E. L. Doctorow's great novel *Ragtime*.

Next came Christopher Wilder, a Florida-based Australian millionaire who from February to April 1984 raped and murdered at least eight women. And, as if this weren't enough, he had the particularly nasty habit of squirting Super Glue in their eyes so that they couldn't identify him. One would think that killing them would have covered that contingency. His end came when a New Hampshire state trooper recognized him as he gassed up in Colebrook. Upon approach, he shot the trooper, and the trooper killed him in his car, right there on Main Street.

The most recent Colebrook tragedy was in 1997 and involved John Harrigan himself. Carl Drega, who lived down in the next town, Columbia, had a tumultuous relationship with authority in general and people in particular. The Colebrook town manager at the time described Drega to me as "a guy who walked around town with big buttons all over him, daring people to push them."

Drega had no truck with civil society—he was a radical libertarian who lived in a personal jungle where any law that ran contrary to his interests was invalid. To his thinking, code-enforcement and land-use laws were patently unconstitutional—so much so they literally drove him to multiple murder.

It started with the tarpaper on his house. A Columbia planning ordinance gives the select board the discretion to determine the reasonable length of time one could claim to be "under construction." A tarpaper facade could be a problem if the house was on a main road, or next to somebody else's house, but that wasn't the case with Drega's. His house was nowhere near the road or anyone else's property.

Despite being told by the police to stay away because it was booby-trapped, I drove down to Drega's house. I didn't trip any traps—the only attack I suffered was purely aesthetic. It looked like the set of red-neck slasher movie. But you couldn't see it from the road. It was across the railroad tracks and down by the river—at least a quarter mile from anything and completely out of sight. You could see it plain as day from the Vermont side of the river, but so what? Nobody in Vermont complained. Still, the official impulse to apply the law evenly doesn't leave a lot of room for exceptions to the rule—especially with a guy like Drega, who reportedly made every effort to be disliked.

Drega had moved to Columbia to escape the planners and zoners of Bow, New Hampshire, where he also lived on the river. For environmental reasons, waterfront property is more closely scrutinized than other parcels and this didn't sit well with Drega.

A riparian zone—the land along a river, lake, or wetland—is the last buffer before the water. The vegetation along a riparian habitat acts as a watershed, catching the run-off from rain and spring melt, reducing flooding. It also filters pollutants—everything from petrochemicals to sewage—out of our drinking water and fish. And even in the absence of mechanical and industrial waste or external pathogens, the quickest way to ruin a good trout stream is to cut down the trees along it. No shade, no trout.

So it isn't without good reason that the government monitors the wet places around us. But, as with most libertarians, the greater good wasn't much of a motivator or mitigator for Carl Drega. He'd hoped for absolute freedom above the notches, but it never went well for him up here. He was often angry and intimidating, which may have been his way, but that attitude will make you friends nowhere, and especially not as a newcomer to a small town. In the end, however, bad manners were the least of it.

The real problems started with the eighty feet of Connecticut River shoreline he filled, saying he was reclaiming a piece of his lot that had washed away in the spring rains of 1981. Unfortunately, the New Hampshire Department of Environmental Services neatly labeled that explanation a lie and accused Drega of trying to change the course of the river. Which will get everyone's attention, including Vermont's.

Drega was ordered to rectify the situation with the aid a licensed engineer and a state-approved plan. A lien would be placed on his property until these conditions were met, and failing to meet them would result in the seizure of his house and land. All this made Drega angrier than a rat on crack.

Vickie Bunnell was a former selectman in Columbia, a part-time district court judge, and a lawyer. She rented space for her law office in John Harrigan's newspaper building—she and John were good friends. A couple of years before the murders, when Vicki was still a selectman, Drega fired shots at her and the town's tax assessor to chase them off his property. He'd been confrontational in slightly more subtle ways, too, so she started carrying a pistol as protection against him. It's not unusual for a man or woman to be strapped around here, but nobody ever really thinks they'll have to use it. Vicki Bunnell labored under no such illusions: she knew Carl Drega.

On August 19, 1997, one of the first warm spring afternoons of the year, Trooper Scott Phillips stopped Drega in the parking lot of the only supermarket in Colebrook. After a brief verbal altercation, Drega reached inside the cab of his truck for the AR-15 hanging in his gun rack and shot Trooper Phillips dead. At that moment, Trooper Leslie Lord, a former Fish and Game officer, pulled onto the scene. Drega fired on his car, hitting him. Lord staggered from the cruiser and fell down, leaning against the left front tire; Drega stepped up and shot him dead.

Drega then stole Phillips's cruiser, drove the quarter mile to John Harrigan's newspaper office, and stormed the front door. Someone had called down to the office to warn Vicki Bunnell and the first thing she had done was to alert the staff, yelling for them to get out of the building. When they were out, she ran out the back door into the parking lot. It's not a large building, so Drega easily skirted the rear, and shot her in the back, dead. Dennis Joos, editor of the Colebrook *News and Sentinel*, tackled

Drega; in a struggle for the gun, Drega shot Joos in the back, killing him, too.

Drega then made the short drive across the state line to Vermont, to the town of Bloomfield, where he perched on a railroad trestle and ambushed New Hampshire Fish and Game Officer Wayne Saunders, causing him to crash his cruiser. The U.S. Border Patrol was called in, and as they and New Hampshire state troopers closed in on the spot where Drega had gone into the woods, he began firing on them from a hilltop, wounding two state troopers and a border patrol agent. After a standoff that lasted well into darkness, Drega was killed by police gunfire.

A couple of days later, the Colebrook town manager told me that Phillips had stopped Drega for having a half-dollar-size patch of rust on the bed of his pickup truck. Drega—paranoid and delusional—saw Vicki Bunnell as a government oppressor and the police as her goon squad. "They found him," the town manager told me, "with a bullet hole in the middle of his forehead. That's pretty good shooting uphill, in the dark."

Like a lot of rural areas, northern New Hampshire attracts a certain antisocial element—those looking to pioneer a wilderness, homestead a plot of land under the supervision of nobody but themselves. You can get pretty close to that ideal up here, but when they learn that we do in fact have rules, that civil society has finally migrated north of the notches, the disappointment underscores their worst fears. In Drega's case, it heightened his already seasoned paranoia into a murderous rage.

John and I drove north along the two-thousand-acre Lake Francis, a reservoir created by Murphy Dam, and he showed me the slightly camouflaged road up into his new hunting camp. Not that he's trying to hide it completely. He just doesn't want kids using it for things it wasn't meant for. Otherwise, he's old-school when it comes to sharing. There's a sign above the unlocked door: USE IT IF YOU NEED IT, LEAVE IT THE WAY YOU FOUND IT. He'd owned the land forever, but just got around to building the camp—there were a number of reasons why he put it off, but primarily it was "the shootings," he said, ten years later, his voice still cracking at the thought.

John drove us up to a piece of land not far from his house that he says, "I reclaimed." That is, he took it back from the encroaching forest, turned into a field again, exposed a very impressive glacial erratic on the back side of it. And he's right—the Great Northern Forest is a jungle that will invade civilization if we allow it. John and I have some of the same implements to beat back the jungle—a Brush Hog (basically a lawn mower on steroids) that will take down a three-inch sapling, weed whackers with razor-sharp steel blades, chainsaws, handsaws, pruning saws . . . it's all about cutting trees and staving off nature.

John says the woods are healthy, that the forest-products industry has little to worry about. The loggers, on the other hand, are more circumspect. Many I know say that the woods are full of pecker poles where there used to be pulpwood in lots of places. The Forest Service's desire to cut in the national forest's roadless areas gives credence to the opinion that if cogeneration electricity plants are going to "save" the North Country from economic ruin (and they'll do no such thing), then new sources of pulpwood must be tapped.

From up high in Colebrook you can see Bunnell Mountain in the Vickie Bunnell Preserve—a 10,500-acre spruce-fir forest and home to more rare and endangered species than any other parcel of land in New Hampshire. And there's the Bunnell Tract—18,680 acres set aside for logging and recreation, and a perfect memorial to Vickie Bunnell's life of public service and enjoying the outdoors. It, too, is a Forest Legacy Program project.

I went way up north and looked for myself to see if the wood could sustain the electrical needs of Massachusetts, Connecticut, and beyond—where most of the electricity generated in northern New Hampshire is likely to go—but covering the top third of the state in an afternoon proved problematic. If not for the scenery and the walk in the woods, it would have been a complete waste of time.

It turns out that trying to figure how much wood is in the forest is almost impossible. You can, depending on whether you're a strict conservationist or a timber-industry economist, tweak the data a half-dozen ways so that in the end you don't even agree with yourself. There are a dozen variables to take into account, five different methods of pricing wood, unknowns such as the rising temperature and the price of oil. The most definitive answer is probably, and some high rollers are building $100 million cogeneration plants based on that probably.

Thousand of acres of trees will be needed annually, but they don't get felled all at once, or all in one place, we hope. Professional forestry practices prescribe a selective cut that first takes the cull wood—diseased, damaged, and misshapen trees—then the low-grade woods, such as balsam fir and beech. Is it always neat and clean in a chipping operation? No, but they're generally the ones you hear about, or notice. The integrity of every timber sale depends on the forester, the logger, and the people who manage the land—whether that's a timberland-management company or a private landowner sitting on twenty acres.

Mistakes are made on every timber sale, but sometimes they are so blatantly illegal that they must be intentional. As I said, these are the ones you hear about and read about in the newspaper for their egregiousness. The thousands of good logging jobs that satisfy everyone just aren't noteworthy. There are forest flatteners out there, but I doubt they see themselves that way. To them, the forest is a crop to be harvested—not flowers to be picked, but hay to be mowed. I've viewed several large clear cuts just after they were completed, when the crime scene was fresh—they were eerie and unfriendly places.

The largest clear cut allowed by law in New Hampshire is forty acres. You can see them from the tops of mountains, like big square scabs on the landscape. The first time I saw a patchwork of clear cuts was from a distant peak. I thought it must be a golf course. But then, I don't golf, so what do I know? It turns out the clear cuts would have added up to three or four very poorly designed eighteen-hole courses.

The upside is that the deer and the brown-tailed bunnies (which are close to endangered) appreciate clear cuts for the undergrowth they create, and the black bears love the wild raspberries. Early successional forest growth is also critical cover and nesting grounds for neotropical migratory birds—those that summer in North America and winter in Mexico, Central, and South America. According to the Migratory Bird Center, the majority are songbirds—warblers and thrushes—plus hawks and waterfowl. I like birds. I love watching the red-tailed and marsh hawks patrol my land, looking for mice. And I mark time by the comings and goings of the ducks and geese. My office is in the woods, and in summer, with the windows open, I hear at least a half-dozen songs outside. What would the forest be without songbirds? A silent movie, I suppose, or at least one without a soundtrack. There is a chickadee that comes back every year to fly into the picture window of my office all day long as I try to work—he thinks his reflection is another bird horning in on his territory. *Him* I'd like to kill. But the rest are as much a part of the forest as are the trees.

After the initial trauma of a clear cut, the forest soon begins to regrow. How well that regrowth goes depends upon how it was left when the harvest was completed.

One clear cut I walked was in the foothills of the White Mountains on the back side of a small mountain just above Newfound Lake. Another was in Twin Mountain. While we can argue the environmental pros and cons of this kind of logging, they were stunning visages of devastation. The woods were all shaved down to the nubs, but not at all like a cornfield after it's been harvested. Unlike the forest, the cornfield was all corn, and next year it will be knee-high by the Fourth of July and as high as an elephant's eye by fall, just as it was last year. Plus, the order and uniformity of a corn harvest is a pleasant sight. But a forest clear cut looks like a burned-out village, sacked and raped and pillaged for each of the myriad organisms it had to offer. It's all stumps and slash—what the biomass industry calls "in-forest residue"—nothing taller than eighteen inches except the odd boulder. The degradation is palpable, a beautiful, living place reduced to nothing. It looks wrong, it smells wrong—muddy and sappy and wet—and it sounds all wrong, too—the birds, the bugs, the chipmunks, the voles . . . all gone. Nothing left to stay for.

Mechanized logging wasn't invented to strip the forest of its trees; it was a safety measure—an attempt to get guys with chainsaws off the ground and inside the reinforced cab of a feller buncher, a monster tractor with giant mandibles that bites the tree off at its base and then drags it away. It's voracious and works faster than a crew of good men on the ground. So, in accordance with the law of unintended consequences, it also changed the nature of logging in ways that have nothing to with safety. An average-size mechanized logging operation requires three million dollars' worth of equipment, and that's a big nut to make every month to the bank. Just moving that much equipment from one job to the next is a serious undertaking. Consequently, it makes financial sense to take as many trees as possible off every job, and sometimes that means every tree.

A former U.S. Forest Service forester once told me, "We do things right, but that's not to say I don't have a few three-hundred-acre clear cuts in my past." A geographically ambiguous comment because that was out west, not in the seven-hundred-thousand-acre New Hampshire National Forest, where a large clear cut is an obvious enormity and hard to justify. The western forests tend to be monocultures—vast stands of the same species of tree. Like cornfields. And for that reason, there are a lot more clear cuts out west. The Great Northern Forest is as diverse as New York City, and only wildlife-habitat creation, laziness, and greed are reasons to log it down to the stumps.

Which brings us to the USDA Undersecretary for Natural Resources and Environment at the time of writing this book—he runs the National Forest Service and the Natural Resources Conservation Service—Mark Rey—a former lobbyist for the National Forest Products Association, the American Paper Institute, and the American Forest Resources Alliance. He was also vice president of the American Forest and Paper Association, which lobbies for expanding logging in the national forests. The White Mountain National Forest is currently approved to produce twenty-four million board feet of logged timber annually, a figure that was arrived at after much research and comment from all interested parties. And it ought to be enough. But not for guys like Mark Rey, whom Robert F. Kennedy, Jr., describes as "the most rapacious timber lobbyist out here."

Except he's not a lobbyist anymore; he's been running the U.S. Forest Service for the last seven years. As a lobbyist he may have helped write the rules, but now he chooses which rules to enforce and which rules to ignore. He learned the politics of timber at the knee of Senator Larry Craig (R-Idaho), perhaps big timber's (ahem) best friend in the U.S. Senate.

On December 23, 2003—a day when most people, if they were thinking of trees at all, were thinking of Christmas trees—Mr. Rey, by administrative fiat, changed the official designation of the Tongass National Forest in Alaska from "roadless," and thus unlogged, to an open-for-business timber sale. A couple of years earlier, fifteen days before his boss, George W. Bush, took office, the Republican-controlled Congress passed the Roadless Initiative, which stopped any new road building in

America's national parks and forests. No new roads meant no new logging areas. But it wasn't just about conservation. The federal government typically loses money on the logging contracts it lets, which even to Congress sounded like a bad deal.

Maybe that's because it was never meant to be a money-making operation. President Teddy Roosevelt created the Tongass National Forest in 1907 for its innate value as a wild and prehistoric place, which was apparent even one hundred years ago. Today, in the era of the megalopolis, the suburbs, the exurbs, global warming, and endangered species, its place in the world is all the more precious.

The Tongass National Forest is the premier temperate rain forest on earth and a rare, untouched corner of the ecosphere within America's borders. Still, the federal government let fifty major timber contracts for the Tongass over the past few years. While only 4 percent of the 17-million-acre wilderness was affected—680,000 acres—there are more trees in the lower forty-eight United States today than there were seventy years ago. Why would we forge into an ancient wilderness that lives and breathes for thousands of species—several that exist nowhere else on earth—rather than use what's readily available and accessible?

Western loggers tend to be more militant about their right to slay any and every tree they meet, but Logger Bob, and every other eastern logger I know, shakes his head and says it's complete bullshit—that there's no reason to log the Tongass when there are so many other working forests providing what the market needs. In fact, most eastern working forests are "productive"—that is, they grow more trees every year than we have an appetite for. True, logging the Tongass means hundreds of local jobs, and that fact's not lost on Bob, Rick, Steve, Mike, or the others. But they respect what the ancient wilderness represents because so little of it exists in the east anymore.

There are several possible reasons why eastern loggers don't support logging in the Tongass (this is not to say that all eastern loggers agree, or that some western loggers don't; the issue cuts along majority lines, like Democrats, Republicans, and abortion). It may simply be the eastern mindset versus the western.

As the U.S. government moved west in the nineteenth and early twentieth centuries, it kept more and more of the land for itself. Oh, it gave plenty away, but the lion's share went to Uncle Sam. Consequently, in the western United States, 72 percent of the land is federally owned—a sort of Big Brother in the woods. Is it any wonder that so many westerners are against big-government conservatives? On the other hand, in the East, where private property is a cultural norm, politics tack left. I have no other data to explain this, but I doubt it's a coincidence. Nevada is 83 percent federally owned, while one-half of 1 percent of the state of Connecticut is; 62 percent of Idaho versus 3 percent of Massachusetts; 68 percent of Alaska compared to 23 percent of Washington, D.C. That's the *District of Columbia,* literally a federal city where they don't even get a member of Congress. There's a trend here.

Secretary Rey's roadless reversal was triggered by a request from the state of Alaska, which came from Governor Frank Murkowski, who, as U.S. senator, hip-waded in the financial largesse of the timber industry and did what he could to roll back roadlessness. But it was upon his election as governor that he formally requested "relief" from the roadless rule. He was obviously feeling his oats, because he also took the opportunity to appoint his daughter to fill out the remaining term of his Senate seat. Even in Alaska, that takes balls.

In the next election, Murkowski was turned out, winning only 16 percent of the vote in his party's primary. Apparently, away from Washington and under closer scrutiny, his welcome wore thin on his longtime constituents. Opening up the Tongass didn't impress everyone, either.

Some people look at an ancient forest and see the past, present, and future all in one place; others see assets, frozen by the U.S. government, screaming for a workaround. The logging concerns with contracts in the Tongass regard all real estate as a material resource, while those who opposed the change see it as sacrosanct—like tearing down the Cathedral of Notre Dame for the salvage rights. There's very little to agree upon.

I tend to agree with the latter perspective, but absolutes make thinking people skeptical. In the end, a good question is always more effective than a great pronouncement. And that question is this: what radical environmental circumstances warrant an elemental reversal of a carefully arrived-at policy? Because the truthful answer is none. There are well-connected logging- and wood-industry concerns that want to cut the old spruce, cedar, and hemlock in the Tongass National Forest, and if that's the only reason, it's not good enough.

In 2006, as a result of lawsuits brought by environmental organizations, the federal courts weighed in on the Bush administration's dismissive attitude toward the roadless rule and reestablished the protections put in place during the final days of the

Clinton administration. The Tongass situation, however, was unaffected by the ruling.

The U.S. Forest Service's 2007 plan for the Tongass in the National Forest Management Act was quickly amended by Congress to end federally funded road building there. The amendment had bipartisan support from environmentalists and budget-conscious conservatives. Estimates put the Tongass logging operation cost to the federal government at thirty million dollars per year. And some estimate that the federal government's sanctioned logging of Tongass over the last twenty-eight years has cost taxpayers one billion dollars—while making Alaskan timber interests very wealthy.

U.S. Representative Steve Chabot (R-Ohio), who sponsored the amendment, said, "I am not opposed to logging when it's done on the timber company's dime. But in this case, they are using the American taxpayer to subsidize these two hundred jobs at the tune of $200,000 per job. That just makes no sense."

Seventy percent of the Tongass's old growth has already been logged. Of the nearly six million acres of the Tongass's remaining potentially commercial forests, only half are shielded from logging. This exposes primeval forests that have never seen a saw or an ax, never had more than a deer run cut through them—truly ancient places. Logging the Tongass is the environmental equivalent of using the Dead Sea Scrolls to wrap your Big Mac.

There are two other spots in the country where the roadless rule is being challenged—Oregon and the White Mountain National Forest. The forest service in New Hampshire adopted a new forest plan in 2005—before the roadless rule was reasserted by Congress. It took nearly a decade to arrive at a document that suited the active stakeholders—the congressional delegation, eight federal agencies, twelve state agencies in two states, fifty-two towns and cities, five Indian tribes, and forty-five organizations. Add to that three thousand written comments, a slew of public hearings, four drafts, and you've got a plan they were loath to rewrite a word of—roadless rule or not.

The White Mountain National Forest advertises itself as the "Land of Many Uses," and it is—primarily logging, recreation, wilderness preservation, and the protection of wildlife habitats. But some people object to the logging. They don't make a distinction between national forests and national parks. Most know the difference between a park and a forest, but that rarely seems to settle the matter in their minds.

The WMNF is nearly 800,000 acres, more than half of which are roadless. There are 281,000 acres considered suitable for logging, largely because of geography. Of those, 94,400 are roadless swaths of burgeoning wilderness set aside for mixed use, which generally means hiking and fishing, and hunting. This is 24 percent of all the roadless area in the state forest.

The plan calls for cutting twenty-four million board feet a year—a 30 percent reduction from the previous plan—which amounts to less than 4,000 acres. Why then are its first seven proposed logging contracts located inside the roadless area, rather than somewhere in the other 183,600 loggable acres?

When it comes to public environmental policy, the New Hampshire chapter of the Sierra Club doesn't like mysteries, so they sued. And in this struggle they find themselves on the other side of the table from the Appalachian Mountain Club, the New Hampshire Audubon Society, the Society for the Protection of New Hampshire Forests, and others. The suit created such a stir that Senator Judd Gregg (R-New Hampshire) denounced the Sierra Club on the floor of the U.S. Senate.

In reality, "inventoried roadless area" is a map label, not a designation. "Roadless" means that no more than 20 percent of a parcel has been harvested in the past decade, and has no more than one-half mile of road per thousand acres. It's meant to indicate areas that may be eligible for "wilderness" designation sometime in the future.

The plan added thirty-five thousand new Wilderness Area acres—these are places where, according to Tom Wagner, White Mountain National Forest supervisor, "The land is in an untrammeled state where man is a visitor . . . and the ecological process is allowed to move on without the heavy influence of man. It's a completely different philosophy from what we use on other multiple-use areas of the forest."

Cathy Corkery of the Sierra Club argues that "designated Wilderness Areas have to be 'small w' wildernesses first." So, again, not a lot of common ground to build on. It's an existential question—preserve the wilderness or create capital. It's the antediluvian against the new world order. To the timber industry "roadless" denotes virgin forest, which means it's just begging for it. Conservationists take a more conservative view of the forest's precious dignity. So the peace talks are over, and it's on to court.

Since it's all in litigation, naturally no one will talk about it, but Corkery says that the groups that support the plan feel they negotiated something worthwhile in it and are afraid that poking it in one place will make it pop out somewhere else. She takes a longer view. She's not antilogging, she's pro-wilderness. As she sees it, there's plenty of room for both, but in separate and distinct areas. That's exactly how the forest service sees it, too. They share philosophies, but differ on the details. Some areas are negotiable, others aren't. The Wild River area is an important watershed and riparian habitat currently in a roadless area. It was last logged in the 1950s, and the forest service thinks it's ready for another harvest. But that's a deal killer for the Sierra Club. And so it goes.

The U.S. Forest Service's decisions are necessarily Solomonic and there are only so many ways to split the forest. In the end, it's a bureaucracy serving many disparate constituencies, and it answers to Washington. The White Mountain National Forest may be in New Hampshire and Maine, but it belongs to Uncle Sam.

Gifford Pinchot, the first chief forester of the U.S. Forest Service, from 1905 to 1910, settled the issue of competing interests in the national forests this way: "Conflict should be decided from the standpoint of the greatest good of the greatest number, in the long run." None of the parties involved found this remark disconcerting because defining the greatest good is always where the rub lies, and, right or wrong, also where politics inevitably steps in to settle things.

The forest service began as Teddy Roosevelt's bully-pulpit response to overcutting, overgrazing, overmining, and the general degradation of much of the nation's forests. Until that time, forestry itself was literally a foreign concept. The first forestry school in America was the Biltmore Forest School, founded in 1898 by Dr. Carl Schenck, George Vanderbilt's forester for his Biltmore Estate. He, and Gifford Pinchot, and any other forester in the United States at the time, had studied in Europe.

In the White Mountain National Forest, overcutting had become an issue that stretched far beyond the trees of New Hampshire and into the water supplies of Boston and beyond. With no trees at the headwaters of the Connecticut and Merrimack Rivers, there was no effective watershed to sift and hold the silt from the runoff when it rained. Suddenly, when they were drinking dirty water on Beacon Hill, the closed-loop nature of the ecosystem became painfully apparent.

It wasn't new science—John Muir, America's premier conservationist, and others had been making these predictions for decades. But the market doesn't start trends, it follows them. Dirty water was bad for business, and the Romantics were painting so many landscapes of the White Mountains and writing poems about them that the railroad laid lines to bring city dwellers north for some fresh air and wilderness experience. Bethlehem, New Hampshire, was known internationally as the "Hay Fever Relief Center of America" and sneezy multitudes flocked there. At one time there were thirty-two luxury hotels in Bethlehem, full of rich flatlanders all summer long.

From this utilitarian need for a balance between beauty and commerce came the concepts of land management and efficient use, the guiding principles for most land-use regulation. In theory, they protect individual and residential property rights, while accommodating commercial use for the maximum benefit of the community. In reality, they provide a basis for inter-minable litigation, rampant and unchecked misinterpretation, and unhappy people on both sides of the street. Which, in a democracy, is how it works.

Teddy Roosevelt's successor, President William Howard Taft—Pinchot's fellow Skull and Bonesman at Yale—fired Pinchot for being too much a tree hugger. So Pinchot and his pals broke away from the Republican Party and formed the Progressive Party, after which Pinchot went home to Pennsylvania and got himself elected governor a couple of times. These same opposing financial and political interests still compete, and as long as there's a forest to fight over, they always will.

And then there are the loggers. While they might support sustainable forestry in the national forest, the small-job loggers can't get in on the business—they're too small, or underinsured, or don't run a sufficiently mechanized operation to qualify to bid on the larger timber sales. Logger Bob went up to look at a recently completed job in the national forest and came back predictably disappointed. "They barked more goddamn trees than I've cut all year," he said. "There's no attention to detail. They got one thing in mind—make their next fifty-thousand-dollar equipment payment. Fast and dirty, the bastards."

Some environmentalists, and most tourists, reject the notion of logging in the national forest at all, claiming that there should be no commercial use of public resources. Timber interests, predictably, don't believe enough logging happens in the national forest. The forest industry wanted a third more cutting in the forest than the plan allows for, or roughly the status quo ante. So, opening up new areas to logging, irrespective of what the roadless rule says, is the point they won in the negotiation. And they're not letting go of it easily.

It's the forest service's job, through policy, to minimize dissent by ensuring that well-managed, judicious logging is a benefit to the forest, just as weeding is for your garden. Logging doesn't have to be a competing interest with environmentalism. Done properly, it's a complement to recreation and conservation.

Just prior to the launch of the U.S. Forest Service in 1905, wild speculation among the timber companies and mills led to vast clear cuts in the White Mountains—many thousands of acres were denuded, multiplying the ecological problems the federal government sought to solve. There are no easy answers as long as wood has value and people cherish the wilderness.

Until it grows up again, a clear cut is a scar, visible from the tops of mountains and by air. There's generally a buffer between the logging operation and the road you drive by it on, so you have no idea what was going on a hundred yards behind that first stand of "beauty strip." Left to its own devices, when a clear cut regrows, it'll be trash trees and thicket; properly managed, it can yield another valuable, more selective, less invasive crop in thirty or forty years.

The wilderness remains vast—thousands and thousands of acres of dense forestland in the impenetrable valleys between mountain ranges, all protected and out of commercial play. In northern New Hampshire, on the windward side of Franconia Ridge, the federal government designated the Pemigewasset Wilderness—all forty thousand acres of it—as a no-roads, no structures, certified wilderness. There are also more stringently

protected areas in the forest, such as the Great Gulf, which requires a permit just to hike in it.

There's one kind of extremist who believes that any cutting
is despoilment. Period. And another who regards all regulation
as an unconstitutional affront to free and fair commerce. These
are the vocal bookends of the argument; the actual majorities on
both sides tend toward the middle ground, where there's still
plenty to disagree about, but also a few important things to accomplish together.

Eighty percent of the Great Northern Forest is privately
owned; less than 20 percent of it is state parks and publicly owned
forests, and only 3 percent of the Great Northern Forest—from
Maine to New York—is owned by the federal government. As
far as the logging industry is concerned, that ought to be
enough. The rest of the forest ought to be logged.

Environmentalists argue that all of the forest is a vibrant,
living, four-season home to millions of living creatures. So harvesting it must be sensible, sensitive, and selective. And if not for
the critters, then for the trees—the forest is a watershed that pro-
tects the valleys against flash floods and filters CO_2 from the atmosphere, reoxygenates it, and keeps us all alive. It's a pretty
nice organic facility here for our use, free of charge. It'd be a
shame to dismantle it as if it were no more than an unwanted
piece of machinery in a closed-down paper mill.

The loggers recognize all this, but ask if it's reason enough
for everyone to live in brick houses with metal framing. With
seven hundred billion acres of forest land in the lower forty-
eight United States alone, should we let it all fall in on itself until it's tinder? Should it become, as Henry David Thoreau once

described it, a ". . . grim, untrodden wilderness, whose tangled labyrinth of living, fallen, and decaying trees only the deer and moose, the bear and wolf can easily penetrate." Or should we wait for lightning to strike some night, or for someone's smoldering love letters to set it all ablaze? And when the fire starts, will it stop before the smoke snuffs out the sun and the flames consume the millions of people who live in the forest?

Common cause/comon sense creeps into the fracas mostly because most loggers are outdoors people—hunters, anglers, trappers, skiers, bikers, hikers. As are conservationists. And they generally live near, if not in, the forest. The independent woodsman working the Great Northern Forest doesn't want his favorite spots encroached upon, his secret fishing hole violated, the oak he built his deer platform in cut down. Nothing motivates like self-interest.

This is the complicated context of the logger's personal and professional life. He operates much closer to the center of controversy than most of us ever contend with. Politically, the average logger dials in at Thomas Jefferson meets Bill the Butcher. Loggers are individualists who are respectful of what is truly larger than themselves—the natural environs we can touch and the universe that we can't. But, in the end, they say let's not get crazy about all that because business is business and there are mouths to feed, bills to pay.

I see both the loggers' and the environmentalists' points of view, depending upon whom I'm with. Except on days when I can see neither side. That was when I was too cold or itchy to think about anything other than that I wished I were writing a book about Central American beaches—especially when I wore my green woolly pants. Prolonged exposure to parched frigid air, no matter how well wrapped you are in wool and down, makes the body itchy and flaky. And while I found it uncomfortable, there was something ennobling about sloughing off so much DNA in this frozen forest and leaving it behind like the ingredients for the next primordial soup. Who knows what might grow?

7

BERLIN

The City That Trees Built

One generation plants the trees; another gets the shade.
Chinese proverb

One of my earliest memories of the North Country is standing on a street corner in Berlin, New Hampshire. Berlin (pronounced with the accent on the first syllable, a conceit adopted in 1917 with America's entry into the War to End All Wars, when sauerkraut became "victory cabbage") is a city of ten thousand souls living north of the White Mountains. It is, by most people's standards, remote—a great place, but not exactly on the way to anywhere.

I was standing on this street corner, watching dozens of heavily loaded logging trucks wend their way through the narrow streets while idly chatting up a longtime native, an elderly man, short and squat, wearing a porkpie hat and brown suit. After telling me about the famous Nansen Ski Jump in town, the German POW camp down the road in Stark during World War II, and what a dick the mayor was, he told that me that his wife had been killed on that very same street corner, right where we were standing. She'd been to the pharmacy and was waiting for her him to pick her up when a logging truck rounded the corner too fast, perhaps to beat the light, and its ten-ton load of softwood snapped its chains and tumbled onto the sidewalk, crushing his wife of fifty-one years.

I stepped back from the curb.

He was retired from the mill, she was a mill worker's wife, and in the days of honey and roses, before the decline of trade unionism, NAFTA, GATT, and globalization, a career at the mill made them middle-class. They had a house full of kids, a car, a camp at the lake, three weeks' vacation, ten holidays, a comfortable retirement, and the knowledge that they and the mill had done important work making things we really can't do without: writing paper, paper bags, and, most of all, toilet tissue—a product that touches everyone.

The city of Berlin is surrounded by hundreds of thousands of acres of forestland, and naturally became ground zero for the logging and the forest industry in New Hampshire. Berlin was a logging camp at the turn of the nineteenth century, and in 1821, a road was built to nearby Gorham, where another paper mill was built. In 1851, the St. Lawrence & Atlantic Railroad cruised into

Berlin; in the early 1850s, Winslow & Company built a state-of-the-art sawmill at the head of the Berlin Falls on the Androscoggin River. All the pieces were there—trees to fell, water to power the mill, an immigrant-labor workforce willing to do whatever had to be done, and a railroad to move the product to market.

In 1868, brothers William and Lewis Brown, whose father owned a half-interest in the mill, bought the Winslow Company outright and renamed it the Berlin Mills Company. Over the next twenty years, more lumber, pulp, and paper mills put down stakes in Berlin. It grew quickly from a logging camp to an incorporated city in 1897. Berlin's city motto is the "The City That Trees Built." That's not exactly "The City That Never Sleeps," or "The City of Lights," but it's better than "Third Oldest City in Oregon." Sorry, Lafayette, but think hard . . . is there anything more you'd like to say about yourself? And the community pressure to brush after every meal in Hereford, Texas, the "Town Without a Toothache," land of the Stepford teeth, must be oppressive. So I always liked "The City That Trees Built"—it impressed me the first time I rolled into town and saw it on the welcome sign. It's a sturdy slogan, and true.

Of course, when the mills were running hard and the smokestacks belched waste, Berlin could have been called "The City That Smells Like the Men's Room at the Bus Station." But so what? Whenever an outsider mentioned the odor to the locals, they'd take a deep breath, smile, and say, "Smells like money!" In fact, that would have been a great city motto, too: "Berlin— It Smells Like Money."

Now the city that trees built is rapidly becoming the city that the trees are reclaiming. The paper industry in northern

New England has sputtered along through bankruptcies, consol-
idations, and massive closures much longer than the smart
money said it would. The arc of creation to destruction took
about two hundred years, but it was nothing out of the ordinary.
Paper mills suffered the same financial slow burn as the rest of
the manufacturing sector experienced starting in the 1960s. Labor costs and environmental mandates, health care costs, work-
place safety requirements—it all eventually made Berlin and its
neighbors uncompetitive.

In 1917, the Berlin Mills Company was renamed the
Brown Company, which, like everything else during the not-so-
great depression, nearly went belly-up. The federal government
stepped in with assistance—to save the jobs, the infrastructure,
and the community. This was the business of government in
those days—to serve and protect, to make the loan that keeps
the town alive. But not anymore. New Hampshire Governor
John Lynch is offering a $1,000 tax credit per position to com-
panies that create jobs in the North Country for $13 dollars an
hour or more. That's $520 a week for forty hours before taxes—
barely subsistence for someone who'd been working at the mill.

Business boomed after World War II—in the 1950s, the
mill employed nearly three thousand people, more than half the
adult population of Berlin. Life was sweet.

According to loggers, the Berlin Mill's penultimate incar-
nation, American Tissue, nearly killed the logging industry in this
part of the state with all the bum checks it passed before going
tits-up in the Androscoggin River. Just before the end, loggers
would race to the bank with a check, hoping to get it cashed before the account was empty again.

American Tissue was sold to Fraser Papers, a Canadian company, and they made one more go of it. Four short years later, in May 2006, Fraser closed Berlin's pulp mill, laid off its final 250 workers, closed the doors, and chained the tall chain-link fence that surrounded the property forever. The cynics in town think Fraser bought it just to put its American competition out of its misery, but Fraser does continue to operate mills in the United States, including northern New Hampshire.

That speculation is fueled by the fact that Fraser sold the 121-acre site, buildings, and equipment for pennies on the dollar to the North American Dismantling Corporation. In twelve short months they deconstructed an era, an industry, and the lifeblood of The City That Trees Built. On a cold and rainy September morning in 2007, the trio of three-hundred-foot-tall smoke-stacks that marked the mill from miles away tumbled down in controlled demolitions, wiping the site clean of its former self.

Hundreds of people watched; the mood was mixed. There were those who saw this as progress, arguing that if the mill wasn't producing jobs or tax revenue, then it was an eyesore and ought to go. Its spot on the river is incredibly beautiful and should be opened up to the public, maybe build luxury condos and beef up the tax base. Something. These were the hopeful mourners—rowdy, but respectful.

Then there was the gloomy group—grim and clearly sad-dened by the loss, hoping right up to the end that something would happen to save the day. But it didn't. They were generally older and less convinced that the future held much promise. They cried, they hugged one another, they turned away as the smokestacks dropped in on themselves.

The forest-fire alarm sounded just before the first one fell, and, as it did, some in the crowd cheered. But not Gerard Lavoie, who had worked thirty-three years in the mill. He called it a "beautiful job," and stood in the light rain and watched as the first two stacks fell like giant trees. He shook his head. "If you worked here," he said, "you got good money. Now we work at Wal-Mart."

The Carsey Institute at the University of New Hampshire interviewed a thousand adults in the Berlin-Gorham area in April 2008 and found most of them doing worse than they had been five years ago—but expecting better days ahead. It's that optimism that keeps people in places like this; but the decline in manufacturing over the last forty years in northern New Hampshire indicates a much less hopeful trend. In 1969, 36 percent of Berlin's jobs were in the pulp and paper mills; by 2005 it was down to 11 percent—and these numbers don't include statistics from the most recent mill layoffs. The median household income for Berlin is $29,647, compared to $49,467 for the state, less than 60 percent of the average.

In 2000, more than 12 percent of Berlin's population lived below the poverty level, which was nearly twice the state average.

Gerard was more than a little misty over this passing. "My father worked at the mill," he said. "My grandfather, too. My grandfather ran the wood shop, my father ran the piping crew."

. The piping crew?

"Anything that got built or installed in the mill got done by the piping crew. My father built it all." His voice quivered with pride and loss, as if he were giving a eulogy.

"I was a welder, and—I'm not bragging here—I fixed anything that was broken. I'm very mechanical. I'd come in at night, Sundays, whatever they needed, and fix whatever was broken. My father built it, I fixed it. It was a beautiful job. I owned my house, boat, cars, vacations . . . now it's welcome to Wal-Mart. One day I have the greatest job, sixty days later I'm fifty-nine years old and unemployed. So I took a job with the demolition company that bought this place for salvage. Cut everything up with my torch, including a new nine-million-dollar boiler. My father built it, I fixed it, then I got to rip it all out. Now that's done and it's Wal-Mart city. I'm a nonreader—I never have been able to read or write. I don't really know why. But where else but that mill could a guy like me have had such a great life?"

This was the second time in six years that the mill had closed. The first time, it laid off 850 workers, when Fraser Papers CEO Mehdi Gabayzadeh was indicted on fraud charges that led to a conviction and a fifteen-year sentence in federal prison. The gist of what he'd done was to dummy up imaginary pulp contracts in order to persuade his bankers to give him three hundred million dollars to stay out of bankruptcy.

Jim Wagner, a third-generation paper maker, was the mill's general manager at the time. "In fifteen years I went through four companies and never changed my office," he said.

Wagner was key in uncovering the fraud, and it was up to him to break the bad news to the employees.

"That was September 10, 2001, just about twenty-four hours before the planes hit the World Trade Center—not a good week in Berlin."

Jim is now the president of the board of trustees of the

Northern Forest Heritage Park in Berlin. There's an interpretive museum in the main house with a lot of rare old logging tools, great photo reproductions on the wall, a touch-screen video presentation set into a pile of logs, and a couple of pairs of spiked boots that look like golf shoes for Goths.

Across the street on the banks of the Androscoggin River is an old-timey logging camp. It's a grouping of low-built log structures—big logs, too, the kind you don't see many of anymore—and a very fair representation of the kind of place that used to keep this town swimming in gravy and Kreme Krisp, the first butter substitute made of vegetable (tree) oil. It came in five-gallon buckets with a packet of yellow dye to mix into it to give it that authentic look.

This and other innovations came from the work of Dr. Hugh C. Moore, an MIT graduate who in 1910 stopped in Berlin to sell a photolytic electric cell he'd invented. Turned out he wasn't doing a hand-over-fist business in the alternative-energy game and was about out of money. So he took a job at the mill until he got back on his feet.

He worked manual labor, yarding logs from the landing to the mill and doing whatever else was heavy and dirty. It didn't take him long to catalog all the inefficiencies he saw—concluding that the mill was wasting nineteen tons of pulp per day. He presented this information to the mill manager, who, duly impressed, put him in charge of enacting the series of changes he recommended. By 1917, Moore had a hundred chemists working for him at the mill, inventing new processes for wood products that revolutionized the industry.

The camp is one of those places that kids get dragged to

and it's all lost on them except the food and lumberjack contest. But some adults have an epiphany—they suddenly get what all the fuss was about when they were kids and got dragged to these places themselves—the realization that people just like us actually accomplished a great deal, built a country, without modern technology. What's more, skilled craftsmen gave their lives to build that country, and it doesn't even exist anymore.

The logging camp features a bunkhouse (The Ram Pasture) and a cookhouse with a sign that reads DON'T SPIT ON THE FLOOR in four different languages because the crew was made up of immigrants—French Canadians, Scots, Poles, Hungarians, Greeks, Irish, English, Lithuanians, Italians, Africans, and more. It was the most diverse culture anywhere outside the big cities—loggers, no matter who they were or where they came from, worked, ate, and lived together.

Maybe because of this, and all the Wobblies running around organizing, Berlin became a politically progressive place. In 1935 it elected a socialist mayor, Arthur J. Bergeron, standard-bearer of the Farmer-Labor Party. The Farmer-Labor guys were good at getting money out of the federal government to keep the mill in business, which was handy during the Great Depression, but in the postwar boom it was no longer necessary. So they faded, but not entirely. Eugene Victor Debs gave a speech in Berlin eighty-some years ago, and when you ask Berlinites about their city today, it sometimes still comes up as a highlight.

The camp cookhouse looks as you'd expect—big room, long tables, lots of chairs. It was run with an iron ladle by the cookee and the first rule was no talking except to ask for something to be passed. Eat up, in and out, there are others behind you, and if there aren't then there's cleaning and preparing for the next meal. The cookee and his helper prepared three to five meals a day for a hundred men—hundreds of pounds of meat and beans and pies, and gallons of "tea so strong you could float an ax in it." The average logger ate seven thousand calories per day—that's about thirty-four jelly doughnuts, close to my limit.

Across from the cookhouse is the Horse Hovel, which is as inviting as the bunkhouse and as tidy as the cookhouse. A blacksmith is next to that, and the boss's office sits at the end of the row. Down below the camp, on the river, is an outdoor amphitheater with a stage in the middle, where the lumberjack shows are held.

I asked Jim Wagner what it felt like to run a giant mill for fifteen years and now oversee a simulacrum—a nonprofit tourist spot that attracts five thousand people a year but doesn't actually produce anything. He smiled and shrugged.

"This is our heritage, the people, the city. This represents our roots, where you come from, how you got here. The mill is gone, the memory isn't."

People are sentimental about the mill. Which I admire, but find astounding because I grew up in a mill family—my grandmother's generation all went to work in the wool mills by the age of ten. My father worked in the wool mill behind our house when I was kid. He took me there when I was about five and I remember putting my mouth on a pipe railing that was encrusted with something nasty; the taste didn't go away until I was fourteen. And what I understood from the adult conversation around me was that the mill was at least a living and God bless us for that. But no more than that. Unless they were close to retirement, everyone wanted out of the mill. So I don't have a lot of warm mill memories. Then I came across this prose poem, written by a Berlin mill worker on a white board at the Heritage museum:

> Good bye old friend, my great-grandparents were with you in the beginning, my grandparents too, walk through life with you, as did my mother and my father, and I'm sure that you remember when my father-in-law left this life right here within your em brace. But it is now good bye old friend because fate has it that I will not pass this way again, always remember that I stayed with you to the end.

Berlin liked its mill.

The city's new industry appears to be corrections—there are brand-new state and federal penitentiaries in Berlin, which unfortunately haven't been the new-jobs windfall the people in town had hoped for; the federal prison won't take anyone over thirty-seven years old for a guard's position. Out of necessity, both facilities drew more from the outside than they did from within the community to fill the ranks.

The Wassau Mill in nearby Groveton closed on December 31, 2007, laid off 300 workers, and shipped its newest paper machine off to Vietnam. Ten weeks later, the Gorham Mill, just past the Berlin city line and owned by Boise Cascade, announced it would lay off 167 workers, nearly 50 percent of its remaining workforce. It has since picked up a pulp contract and won't have to lay off as many workers. For now.

The decline began forty years ago and accelerated rapidly

over the last twenty. Global competition, relatively high labor costs, rising fuel prices, and mega-agribiz tree farms out west ate away at northern New England's market share. In response, the mills became tighter ships, running for years on loans and local survival instinct. Union and management knew that without one, the other would have no purpose, so everyone worked hard to hold on to what they had. Mill towns often mimic the mechanization of their focal point, and Groveton and Berlin were no different. The local government worked closely with the mill— not exactly a cog in the wheel, but definitely the grease that kept it from grinding to a halt. The town relied on the mill for the lion's share of its tax base and jobs for the rest of its taxpayers. The smaller businesses in town—the bank, restaurants, video store, dry cleaner, hardware store—all relied on the mill to generate income for their customers. No mill, no nothing.

After the Berlin mill announced it was closing, virtually every other business in town stopped hiring. Applicants were told, "We're waiting until the mill closes before we fill any new positions." The mill was the land in a farming town, the pier in a port town, the Grand Canyon in a tourist town, and the people with the expertise to run the economic engine of the town need to be taken care of first. You can call it insular, or unfair, or small-town to a fault, but the people in Berlin think what's right is to do well by your neighbors, to protect one another when life skips the rails.

There was never any dispute about whether the mill was a good thing. It was a great place to work. It could be a physically demanding and sometimes complicated job—from wood buying, to pulp making, bleaching, and paper production, there was a narrow profit margin to limn and tight quality controls to maintain. At their height, the mills ran two shifts a day and four paper machines at a time. The mill was a team and the goal of the game was to stay in business. It worked for a while. But globalization and free trade agreements have been hard on America's manufacturing sector. Gerard Lavoie told me that his boss on the demolition job at the mill was off to a new job in Illinois to tear down a Chevrolet plant. "He said, damn, I'm from Detroit, the last thing I want to do is take down an auto plant."

What's hardest to replace is the community—that America has a huge wood-products economy, that people rely on wood in ten thousand different ways, and that for their entire history until now, the people of Berlin were an important piece of that wood culture.

According to everyone from the Natural Resources Defense Fund to the paper industry, the average American uses between 700 and 741 pounds of paper per year. Maybe the discrepancy comes in how much toilet paper certain individuals use and how many paper coffee cups they discard in a week. It's a moving target, a big one.

According to TAPPI, the worldwide Technical Association of Pulp and Paper Industry, "Every year, Americans use more than 90 million tons of paper and paperboard. That's an average of 700 pounds of paper products per person each year. Every year in America, more than 2 billion books, 350 million magazines, and 24 billion newspapers are published."

Which is impressive. But Oberlin College's recycling program breaks it down from the forest's point of view: one ton of 100-percent virgin newsprint uses twelve trees; a pallet of twenty-weight copier paper contains forty cartons and weighs one ton; one tree makes 16.67 reams; one ream—five hundred sheets—uses 6 percent of a tree.

One ton of coated, high-end virgin magazine paper that you see in magazines such as *National Geographic* requires fifteen trees to produce; one ton of coated, low-end virgin magazine paper, used by news magazines and catalogs, takes nearly eight trees. Each and every one of us uses two mature pine trees' worth of paper products every year. Together, we use fifty million tons of paper annually—that's more than 850 million trees. Americans discard 80 percent of the office paper we use every year—that's four million tons—enough to build a twelve-foot-high wall of paper from New York to California. But it doesn't come from Berlin, New Hampshire anymore. Those days are gone.

Public Service Company of New Hampshire expressed a strong interest in retrofitting the Berlin Mill to a fifty-megawatt cogeneration biomass, converting wood chips to electricity, like its plant down on the seacoast. But state law required legislative approval for PSNH to increase its energy output. The legislature declined to do so, largely because some powerful members felt that the competition might be healthy. New Hampshire pays the highest electricity rates in the country, so it was hard to argue the point. It wasn't long before another player with the wherewithal to fill PSNH's shoes made a bid for the project, and soon another wanted to do the same with the Groveton Mill. All of this would be good news except the projects are temporarily on ice. Apparently, the electrical transmission lines in this part of the state are inadequate to pump more than one hundred megawatts of power.

That's right, we're underpowered—an economic backwater, a frozen third-world colony left to flounder in 1960s infrastructure and technology. This not only explains the dearth of jobs, it's also the reason why so few of us have access to DSL lines and cable. The lady at the cable company told me that everybody else would have holo-decks, like on *Star Trek,* before the company will run a line all the way up my hill. Consequently, my Internet connection is a satellite dish, and when it snows or rains really hard, like it does a lot lately, it runs like an arthritic dial-up.

What's worse is that the dish is on my work shed, a two-story structure meant to look like a giant birdhouse. My wife liked that building more than all the others when we moved in, and then I hung a satellite dish on the front of it. It was the only place we could get a signal. She frowned when she saw it.

"Hey," I told her, "it's the North Country, we all have to sacrifice."

Speaking of sacrifice, if they're not going to make toilet paper here anymore, then to hell with toilet paper. Who needs it? Let's move to a more civilized bidet system. According to Tree Hugger.com, Americans use 36.5 billion rolls of TP every year—that's fifteen million trees, 4.7 billion gallons of water, and 253,000 tons of chlorine to bleach the wood nice and white. The bleaching part is a mystery to me. Perhaps they should focus-group this, because I bet a lot people would buy brown toilet paper if they thought it was better for the environment. They could probably even charge more.

The whole country uses four thousand terawatts of electricity every year—every residential, commercial, industrial, and public use—and the tree-to-toilet-paper manufacturing process eats up more than seventeen of those terawatts. Which doesn't even include packaging or transportation. So TP production is sizable in terms of energy consumption—somewhere between Starbucks latte machines and downloading porn.

Toilet paper is designed to break down quickly—as anyone who has used it can attest—but as treatment capacity lags behind population growth, TP residue clogs municipal sewer systems and water-treatment plants. It also raises hell with septic systems if they're not pumped regularly—which means more trucks for disposal.

But if we all installed bidets—think of it—the toilet paper business would be brought to its knees. It's just a fantasy, of course, and a bitter, mean-spirited one at that, but I'd like to see the world's largest bidet factory located in Berlin. That'd teach them to screw with the North Country.

The current scheme is to turn New Hampshire trees into electricity somewhere else out on the great grid. Nationally, there are 110 wood-burning cogeneration plants and they're where the trees are. If chips are trucked more than ninety miles, the power they generate quickly becomes either unaffordable or unprofitable. Currently in New Hampshire there are 118 megawatts of electricity powered by five wood-chip-burning plants, and three more projects in the design phase for 150 megawatts more. But will they happen in time to save the logging industry? It's a four-year process from concept to output. That's a lot of down time for a logger with a ten-thousand-dollar-a-month feller-buncher sitting idle. After all those guys have gone out of business and gotten jobs running heavy equipment, selling heavy equipment, or stealing heavy equipment, still—if they build it, will they come? Will they be back in the woods cutting and hauling wood? Yes, they will.

8

WOOD POP

Birlers, Carvers, and Comics

---

*It's all fun and games until someone
loses an eye . . . then it's fun and games
you can't see anymore.*
James Hetfield

Trees—the wood they produce and the
forests they comprise—are firmly rooted not just in
our history and economy but, most important, nearly
everywhere in our culture and our language. Living in the
second-most-forested state in the nation with a long tradition of
logging, trees pop up in some odd places. On April Fool's Day
2008, New Hampshire Public Radio ran a story about a stand of
square trees that had been selectively developed by a forester—
easier to stack, less waste when they're milled; square trees

promised to be the latest and greatest innovation in the forest-product industry. It was a good gag, but embarrassing when the station started getting phone calls from high school science teachers wanting to bring their classes out on a field trip to see them. Can you even comfortably hug a square tree?

Then there was the case of James Coldwell, who allegedly had the brilliant notion in July 2007 to rob a bank in Manchester disguised as a tree. He duct-taped leafy sticks to his head and arms, entered the Citizens Bank on Elm Street, and demanded cash from the teller. It's not as strange as it sounds—it was a branch office, after all, and there's never any telling how far out on a limb some guys will go to get what they want.

Logger language often finds its way into the popular lexicon. I like to think of it as the rap of the woods. "Peckerhead," for instance, came from the loggers who saw the damage a woodpecker could do to a tree. They find them a lot less cute than the rest of us do.

We've discussed "skid row," and frankly the loggers will probably never live that one down. Then there's "log jam," which is almost never a good thing, and "loggerheads." The etymological jury is out on whether "loggerhead" has anything to do with loggers. Its first use, according to the *American Heritage Dictionary*, was in 1588, probably from dialectical *logger*, meaning "A blockhead; a dolt." Later, it meant "a thick-headed iron tool," a type of cannon shot, and, since 1657, a type of turtle. "Loggerheads" or "fighting, fisticuffs" is from 1680. "At loggerheads" meaning "in disagreement" dates back to 1831. It sounds like it could have its origins in logging, but there's no hard evidence to prove it.

But do we know that the "grease monkey" was the guy who *greased the skids*—there's another crossover phrase, used mostly by politicians and real estate developers, often during the same discussions—with rendered animal fat so that the logs could roll on and off the skids more easily? This was long before the industrial revolution and the invention of big greasy machines.

"Heads up!" comes directly from logging for obvious reasons. It literally means look up, because if a tree is coming your way, that's where you need to notice it—not when the trunk is six feet from your forehead and falling. It's also a good way to notice broken branches dropping out of trees, perhaps the worst hazard in the woods.

"Haywire" refers to the light rope used for myriad things on old logging jobs. It usually involved jury-rigging something, which would inevitably break and make more trouble. It was used as an adjective, as in "Haywire outfit," meaning a lousy logging crew, and as a verb, as in "haywire the job," meaning doing it on the cheap. The subtext is that if you hire a haywire crew, or haywire the job, things will go terribly wrong. *Haywire.* How much of life does that neatly describe in a single word?

"Windfall" has its roots in logging—but a blown-down tree is usually a nuisance, maybe a hazard. It's broken or uprooted and needs to be hauled out of the way. But "windfall" has come to mean a financial boon you didn't have to work for at all—like "I never touched it, the wind blew it down." But that doesn't describe a windfallen tree—not to anybody who's worked in the woods, anyway.

"Logrolling" is a term that has half retained its original meaning—logrolling among associates now means to work on one another's behalf to achieve a quid quo pro. Logrolling in the river-drive sense was two river runners working the same log in the water to get it to go in the same direction. Not a quid quo pro, but a shared goal. It required perfect timing and focus. Now it means writers writing blurbs for one another's books (guilty), politicians cutting deals, and basically any transaction where one hand washes the other.

The sport of logrolling takes the original purpose of logrolling and turns it upside down. It's a sport that puts two people on a log who are each trying to knock the other off—a duel that will only end when one of them is very wet.

Then there's "fire in the hole!" which was used while blasting log jams in the river free with gunpowder charges—the explosive equivalent of "heads up." It's now, sadly, a mere euphemism for flatulence. My nine-year-old son gets a lot mileage out of it.

The first standout example of a logging character in the popular culture is Paul Bunyan. That's if you don't count the Woodsman in "Little Red Riding Hood," which was a supporting role at best. But I'm biased. *The Adventures of Paul Bunyan and Babe the Blue Ox* was the first book I ever owned. I picked it up and it struck me as if it were something holy or official. It was big like a dictionary or a Bible and had a drawing of Paul and Babe on the cover. We were in a toy store and my father wanted to buy me a GI Joe, but I saw the book and for the first time in my life it occurred to me that I could actually own a book. I remember the odd look on my father's face, as if I'd asked for a Barbie doll. Still, he did buy me the book.

The first stories about Paul Bunyan came from a newspaperman, James MacGillivray, in 1910, written in the prairie fabulist style of the early Mark Twain. He took lumberman lore and embellished it—the lakes of Minnesota, for instance, were created by Paul and Babe's footsteps. Paul dug the Grand Canyon by dragging his ax through Arizona (somehow missing Sedona). But Paul and Babe truly entered the popular consciousness—as conscious as anyone who reads stories about giant lumberjacks is likely to be—when an advertising copywriter, William Laughead, got hold of the Bunyan myth and put it to work for the Red River Lumber Company through a set of pamphlet-size books, the first entitled "Introducing Mr. Paul Bunyan of Westwood, California."

When towns from Bangor, Maine to Westwood started claiming Paul as their own, a new myth developed that he had been born (by five storks) in Bangor, but after flipping his raft in the Bay of Fundy, creating a seventy-five-foot tsunami and some really pissed-off fishermen, his family packed him up and moved to Minnesota. Where, presumably, there was ample room for rampant destruction. Other versions have him moving to the West after he'd cut down all the trees in the East, which rings much truer.

And that was pretty much it for lumberman literature until 1964, when Ken Kesey published *Sometimes a Great Notion*. A great book. It's the story of the Stamper family, a clan of loggers whose motto, "Never Give an Inch," comes in handy as they fight to stay in business against the onslaught of trade unionism and the chainsaw. More than forty years after the book's publication, the technology has caught on much better than the organizing. Loggers and unions are like onions and ice cream, the

American Loggers Council claims it "serves the interests and promotes the professionalism of over 50,000 loggers," but nobody I know has anything to do with them. And the Modern Woodmen of America, despite sounding like a 1980s skinny-tie band, is a life insurance company.

The title of Kesey's novel is a snatch of lyric from the Lead Belly tune "Goodnight, Irene": *"Sometimes I live in the country, Sometimes I live in the town, Sometimes I get a great notion, To jump into the river an' drown."* The 1971 film starred Henry Fonda and Paul Newman; Newman also directed. It was the last great logging movie. Actually, the only great logging movie. Aside from some documentaries about logging in Maine and Florida made at the turn of the twentieth century, theatrical shorts, cartoons, and a few prologging agitprop films made to blunt the complaints of environmentalists in the early 1990s, there haven't been many logging films made. Except, perhaps, "Lumberjack of All Trades: The Bigfoot Massacres" (2006), the plot synopsis of which reads: "Mark the Lumberjack is a woodsman with a bad temper and an even worse drinking problem," there's a dearth of logging film fare. Which is puzzling when you consider the narrative, character, and cinematographic possibilities.

Logging has found its way to the small screen in a big way. "Ax Men" on the History Channel is a three-ring-circus documentary look at Oregon loggers, focusing on the screwups and bad luck of several different crews through the three-month logging season. It's all snapped cables, mud-mired yarders, near-miss decapitations, and the hardest work anybody anywhere does outside a war zone. Naturally the producers had to make it a contest between the crews, featuring a graphic charting the number of loads each trucked to the mill that day—a sort of *Survivor* with chainsaws. Except it's all real, or at least as real as TV gets.

There's a weekly TV show on one the networks, which one I couldn't tell you, called "Men in Trees," starring Anne Heche. I don't have a TV, so if I can't buy or rent something on DVD, I just don't see it. I asked Logger Bob (who does have a TV) about "Men in Trees" and he nearly bit my head off.

"Goddamn soap opera," he spit. "It's not about logging." So I left it at that.

If by popular culture we mean "of the people," actual chainsaw carving is the most ubiquitous art form wood takes, with the possible exception of celluloid film, which, while also made from wood, few of us recognize it as such. But if you're like me, when you take a drive in the country you eventually ask yourself, "What's with all the carved bears for sale on the side of the road?" To find out, I stopped and asked.

Mike is the proprietor of a roadside statue garden. As I approached him, he was helping a woman load a piece of wooden sculpture—a six-foot raccoon—into the back of her shiny SUV. Mike is as bearish as a human can be without ending up as somebody's trophy rug. He says that he, like any other sculptor, was called to make his art.

"To transform the ordinary into the extraordinary."

He's drawn to the medium (tree stumps) and the tools (chainsaw, chisels). The bears he carves aren't the cuddly Teddy variety. His are more lifelike, fearsome, and generally up on two legs, looking to take care of business. Mike carves a lot of human figures, too—some more representational than others, all of them interesting. There are men, women, Uncle Sams, Indian braves, African medicinemen, all of which seem to carry a residual spark of treelife. For all I can tell, the seven-foot Paul Bunyon might give me a whack.

"If you plan to make a living at this," Mike told me, ". . . the bears are your bread and butter." His creations sit on a well-traveled state highway between Concord and Portsmouth, and, according to him, the suburban appetite for wooden folk sculpture grows every year. "I spend winters carving them and the rest of the year selling them," he said, smiling.

Ray Murphy of Hancock, Maine is the quintessential "Chainsaw Sawyer Artist," and jumped-up Jesus, whatever you do, don't call him a sculptor. He claims to have invented chainsaw carving in 1953 by carving a squirrel face on a fence post. To this day he uses a chainsaw and nothing but a chainsaw.

"These guys who call themselves chainsaw carvers—they're using chisels and drills and these little damn Dremel tools. That's not chainsaw carving, that's wood sculpting. To me, there's an obvious difference." He pulled an old, yellowed newspaper clipping of some guy carving a duck with a small, specialized tool I'd never seen before.

"Look at that," he said. "Read it. It says, 'With chainsaw in hand . . .' Chainsaw in hand—that look like any chainsaw you ever seen?" It did not.

"That's the kind of pathetic crap I got to put up with. You'd think a journalist would know better, but no. They bastardized an art I love and invented, and nobody cares. I'm an old logger, and I'd like to see those guys go out on a logging job with their grinders and sanders and see how much they get done.

They call their work 'hand-carved'—using a power tool is not hand-carving. These people have ruined it for the real hand-carvers and chainsaw artists. They ought to call themselves 'power tool carvers,' but that don't have much ring. A chainsaw has a romantic side to it that a grinder lacks. Guys like me made it popular and now they're coming along and reaping the gravy. They use me, whose reputation is far-flung around the world, to build their business because they can't do it themselves."

So now I know I'm in the company of true genius, because an amateur or a weekender just does his thing and doesn't worry about anyone else, but a real artiste, in my experience—whether a painter, poet, or sculptor—spends at least as much time ripping the shit out of other people's work as he does praising his own.

Ray first hefted a chainsaw when he was ten years old; fifty-five years and more than fifty-four thousand carvings later, he's migrated from his native Wyoming to Downeast Maine, near Bar Harbor. Earlier in his life he was making a go of it in the woods, but logging is a tough business and, as it often does, a bit of bad luck put him under.

"One year I did so well that the next I doubled my crew, bought all new equipment, and then we all just set there looking at each other. I don't think anybody bought a single stick of wood that year.

"I can't even be a logger no more. They won't let me in the woods 'cause I can't pass their test. Don't even want to take it. You have to go to classes and learn how to fell trees proper and whatever else they got you doing these days."

Ray is missing parts of three fingers on his right hand—I

think it's three fingers; I tend to wipe that stuff from my memory before I write it down, and in my mind his whole hand is mangled. He didn't lose them logging, but the vagaries of logging were involved.

"I couldn't get into the woods in spring. This was between my junior and senior year of college and I needed to make some money to go back to school. My specialty is timber felling, that's what I did to make a buck. But it was rainy, rainy, mud season lasted way up into June. So I had to work somewhere, and the lumber mill was there. Then one day I put my hand where I ought not have and that's how the fingers came off. But losing these fingers is a benefit to me. Anytime you get a handicap, there's some offset, some benefit. Every kind of bad brings some kind of good. Me, I learned to write with my left hand, in fact I learned to do everything left-handed. And that's why I can do the double saw cuts in the show. It's a very steady trigger finger for the saw [there's one knuckle left of his right index finger] and I don't have to use any extra muscles, no extra thinking, which gives my brain time to do other things. People are kind of shocked when they hand me change and it just falls on the floor—that sort of embarrasses them, and I feel bad about it, but you just have to snicker. Oh, and it makes getting a hold of nuts and bolts to put them together kind of difficult. That's a hindrance, but all in all, I try to see the positive in everything."

And then he snickered.

At his shop on Route 1, the twelve-foot sign out front reads: THE RAY E. CHAINSAW SAWYER ARTIST™. The lot is a swarm of carvings—bears, bunnies, garden trolls, fishermen, moose,

ducks, woodpeckers; a couple of dozen white pines and hem-
locks stand on their ends to dry, preparing to reveal their inner
bears. I found Ray out front in the hot sun with a hand pump
sprayer squirting another coat of polyurethane on a new batch
of carvings, all of them, except a soaring eagle as big as a
Barcalounger, set on poly-encrusted cable-spool tables. He turned
and smiled at me and I saw immediately that this was one imp-
ish character. He had the look—a slimmed-down Santa with long,
wispy white hair and beard, a snappy smile, and the smoothest,
pinkest skin I've ever seen on a man in his sixties. Or, for that
matter, one in his forties.

When he'd finished spraying, we went inside his self-built
gallery and jawboned about this and that until suddenly a giant
hornet—I mean the size of a small bird—cruised in through the
open door.

"Oh jeez," Ray said. "I have to shoo that thing out before it
stings a tourist. Because that's trouble. One time, a woman was
in here and the wind blew some dust in her eye. I felt bad and
told her she ought to go down to the Doc in a Box and have her
eye flushed. Then her friend says, 'You ought to sue the bastard.'
That's when I pointed to that saw with the four-foot bar in the
corner over there and said, 'That's my insurance policy. Anybody sues me for something I didn't do and I'll take them out at
the legs, make sure they never enjoy a nickel of my money. And
I'll do their lawyer, too.' That ended all talk of lawsuits."

Okay, I thought. A little harsh, but guaranteed to keep the
riffraff and grifters away. And on a warm summer day on Route
1 in Maine, you're bound to see your share. Ray isn't about to be

cheated out of his life's work—the primary asset of which is a shopping center-size location on a busy strip of the main thoroughfare of "Vacationland."

"Developers have tried to buy this lot from me," he said. "And for big, big money. But I won't sell—not now, anyway, I'm having too much fun. I don't even have to be out here, dealing with the public, doing the show. I have two hundred fifty collectors who buy a piece from me every year. I could make my living just off that, but like I say, I'm having too much fun."

A logging truck loaded to capacity hit its jake brake as it went by us; jake brakes use the engine's compression to slow the truck and make a loud bang and hiss when they pop. A lot of logging towns have prohibitions on using them inside the city limits because they're so annoying.

Ray eyed the load and said, "All that yellow birch, maple, and oak looks like firewood to me. I watch them come and go all day long. You can see what's happening in the woods right from here. The bud worm came through and hit the spruce hard, there's a blight on the fir—aphids, I believe—that's causing them to cut them when they're still small. They cut trees these days like they're mowing them down; it's hard on the ecosystem. There's some disease affecting the tamarack, too, I don't know what it is. I suppose someday they'll all be gone, like the working man, the skilled laborers who know how to build and fix things, the pride-and-joy craftsmen, the old timber fellers who know how to take care of the woods. All gone. I'm trying to see the positive side to that, but it's a tough one."

Ray made the first "chainsaw art" in 1953, sold his first piece in 1960, logged around the United States and Canada for three years, went to the University of Wyoming for a degree in forestry, worked as an ironworker, competed in lumberjack competitions in which he set three world records, and, in 1979, chainsawed the alphabet on a number 2 pencil for the first time.

At the other end of the compound was a new metal building where the "World's Number One Chainsaw Sawyer Art Stage Show" takes place nightly, all summer long. Travel guides and tourist maps cite Ray as a don't-miss destination. He may be the inventor of chainsaw carving, but he's also a marvel and a showman who's been featured on "Ripley's Believe It or Not," ABC's "Wide World of Sports," "The Old Farmer's Almanac," and "All Things Considered." He was turned down by *The Guinness Book of World Records* because only feats of a competitive nature are allowed in the *Guinness Book* and no lines were forming to carve the alphabet onto a pencil with a chainsaw.

The night I saw Ray's show there was a small house in the bleachers for four hundred—just me and a young couple on vacation from New York City. He ran a jazz bar on 119th Street, she didn't say much, but they smiled a lot. They liked Ray's show. By Manhattan standards it's a hell of a lot of entertainment for ten bucks.

"This place is usually pretty packed," Ray said, "but everybody's down at the auto races tonight." Sounded reasonable, probably true, and in the end, who cares? Pearls before swine, I say.

The announcer, a gangly kid with long hair, big glasses, and a mellifluous speaking voice told us over the loudspeaker that "Ray invented the chainsaw sawyer show because he's getting some age on him and feels he should share his talents with the world before it's too late." That's a fairly common urge, or delusion, depending on the person and the talent. I can certainly relate to it, but I have no idea which category I fall under. Ray has no doubts—he's a self-made and proclaimed master wood sawyer artist.

When the show begins, he stands at the far end of the building inside a soundproofed booth with a large picture window in the front. It looks like a recording studio, except the idea is to keep the sound in, not out. The announcer says, "The show you are about to see is like nothing you've ever seen because there's no one else on the planet capable of doing most of these feats. Ray was born in Fort Washington, Wyoming and was raised on the Wind River Indian reservation. His mother was Shoshone, his father was Irish, and by the age of ten, Ray was very good with both an ax and a cross-cut saw. He also started using chainsaws when he was ten, and created the first piece of chainsaw art—a squirrel—when he was eleven years old. In 1976, Ray entered a competition , which he won, in which he made a chair in twenty-eight seconds, a squirrel in eighty-nine seconds, and twenty-seven sculptures in eight hours."

At this point I thought the guy might get fired for calling them "sculptures," but he went on, "For four years after that, Ray traveled the country working for various chainsaw companies demonstrating the capabilities of their saws. He quit this in 1980 and since then has had no part of any corporate structure. In 1979, Ray sawed the alphabet on a pencil for the first time. People had tried it, but Ray was the first to successfully accomplish it."

Ray fired up a saw; despite the soundproofing, it was still

loud. When he works with a chainsaw in each hand, in a big metal building, without the thick glass and the damping in the walls of the booth, it would sound like the space shuttle taking off. Later, tapping the glass, he told me, "Same bulletproof stuff they use in banks."

A video camera is mounted on the ceiling inside the booth, zoomed in to show the detail work on the flat-screen TV hanging above the viewing window. And there's a lot of fine detail work. His first feat of chainsaw wizardry is to carve a bijou chair from a small block of wood in ten seconds or less. It's a slick move. When he sets to work, he looks like a wizard inside his charm room—moving purposefully and quickly, examining pieces of wood for their potential, positioning the work so that it can be seen by the camera, tinkering with his saws. He wants it to all happen without a hitch, but it is art after all, not engineering, and every show is different. This is delicate work and the audience appreciates that fact immediately. At least the three of us that night did. And then suddenly, to the tune of "It's in His Kiss," Ray carved up his second work of the night. In less than two minutes he turned two blocks of wood into a reasonably appetizing hamburger and a pile of French fries.

Ray says there's a big difference between "stunts" and what he does, which is a demonstration of "talent and skill." For this reason, he trained himself to carve the alphabet and numbers "1" through "15" on a Popsicle stick. (He's gotten as high as "16.")

He paints the sticks black because the carvings would be difficult to see otherwise. Then he tacks them down on a stump with small rivets. As he cuts, he makes his marks by barely touching the moving blade to the stick, the tiniest little ticks here and there, and suddenly another number, another letter, emerges. You can't imagine the light touch this requires, the countless hours spent with Popsicle sticks, a chainsaw, and Aretha Franklin belting out "Respect." Nobody ever considers the time and practice that goes into perfecting a talent like Ray's. I have a friend, Roland, who did high-end wood turning until the sawdust from exotic woods got to his lungs. These were works of art, featured in *Fine Woodworking* magazine and juried by all the chichi craft shows in the country. He sold them for $500 to $750 apiece, sometimes more. And buyers, Philistines that they are, often asked how long it took him to produce.

"Three hours, maybe a little longer," he says.

"Whoa," the really obnoxious ones, usually a $500-an-hour attorney, would say. "You make $250 an hour?"

"No, I don't," Roland would reply. "Ask me how long the first one took."

Ray finished carving the alphabet on the Popsicle stick and brought it out to show us, peering at it in the dim light to judge his craftsmanship.

"Oh jeez," he said. "I forgot the *M*."

"Your name is *Murphy*," I pointed out.

"Well, you know, your mind is ten miles away," he said. "Thinking about other things, you make mistakes, dontcha?"

Yes, you do, and that's how most chainsaw accidents happen. This one, by comparison, was a small one.

"I make mistakes all the time," said the woman from New York.

"By golly, a woman who admits to makin' mistakes.

Where'd you find her?" Ray asked the man from New York. "You got a good eye. What's your name, darlin'?"

"Maria," she said.

He headed back into the booth and started in on carving a pencil—many of which, the announcer told us, have sold around the world to museums and private collectors. But when he was done, instead of carving the alphabet onto the pencil, he carved "Maria" on it. Then he sharpened it with his chainsaw, but the graphite kept breaking and it took three tries. It was a perfectly pointy pencil when he was done.

"That's what's happened to good old American pencils," he said. "They're made in China now and an old logger like me has to work three times as hard to make a living because of it."

Next up was a volunteer to wear a wooden belt buckle around his waist as Ray carved his name into it. There being only three people in the audience (the take for the night was thirty bucks, which I figure he paid his announcer with), I stepped up.

I stood inside the booth with Ray while he swept the place, as if I'd just stopped by unexpectedly. But he was right, it wasn't nearly as neat inside as it looked from outside and needed a quick tidying. He put down the broom and handed me my ear protection—the only kind of protection I got.

As he strapped the thick brown leather belt around me, affixing it with a three-inch by two-inch simple wooden belt buckle, he said, "This shirt's going to get all oily. Ruined."

I shrugged. The shirt was the last thing on my mind. I must have looked nervous because he asked me if I was sure I wanted to do this. Or maybe that was a logger's version of a disclaimer. I told him I wasn't worried, I'd already had a vasectomy.

"That puts my mind at ease, too," Ray said, smiling that smile, pink cheeks all puffed up, jollylike. Then, after six excruciating pulls on the chainsaw, my nerves rattling, anxiously waiting for the loud whine inside the little hermetically sealed space—the smell of bar oil and sawdust filling my sinuses, the bright lights burning my eyes—finally the saw yawped and grizzled to life. Ray faced me, winked, and just did it. Exactly the way it went with my V-job.

Well, not exactly. Immediately the tip of the saw vibrated my belly and sent tingles all down through my nethers. Frankly, it wasn't all that unpleasant. It took just thirty seconds, but felt like thirty minutes. He handed me the buckle and I stumbled back out into the audience of two, feeling as though we'd been through something together. They were laughing their asses off. So was Ray.

When I got home from the trip I told my nine-year-old son about the experience—not so much the tingly-pelvis part—and he stood in the kitchen bug-eyed, listening to my feat of incredible courage, laughing, cringing, his lower lip curled in semi-mock fear.

When I was finished he said, "Seems to me, Dad, that if he put your name on it, you ought to have been able to keep it."

"Ahh," I said, "but he didn't put my name on it," and I held the belt buckle out to him with his name, Liam, chainsawed into the wood. He whooped with delight, grabbed it, hugged me, and ran upstairs to put it with all the other weird stuff I've found for him. You'd have thought I'd bought him a Wii.

The show's grand finale is Ray carving a lightning bolt, the moon, and the stars simultaneously, with two saws. He reminded me of Max Roach, who could play the drums with all four limbs doing completely different things.

Then Ray came out and did a little stand-up comedy. He told the one about the priest, the rabbi, and the preacher walking across the lake, and then how many Polish guys does it take to screw in a lightbulb . . . he's a lot more entertaining with a chainsaw. I told the one about how the toothbrush was invented in Maine—if it had been invented anywhere else, they'd have called it the teethbrush. I could say that because there weren't many Mainers in the room.

Ray cuts fast with a sharp saw and soft wood, and, like anyone who's really good at what he does, he makes it look easy. But it's not. To others who work with a chainsaw all day long, what Ray does isn't even believable without seeing it. I told Logger Bob about Ray and he said, "Yeah, that's bullshit." I just left it at that.

I made a date to meet Ray at his shop the next morning. My motel was up Route 1 a bit, and when I tried to get back down to Ray's after breakfast, I found the road was closed. Somebody in an SUV had had a head-on collision with a logging truck and people were dead. So I got detoured around some lake on some hellacious road with no idea where this reroute was going to dump me on Route 1, when I came to a T intersection and saw Ray's shop about hundred feet south of me.

I hung around the shop for a couple of hours, chewing the fat. Ray told me about his logging accidents, which weren't too bad. Some cuts and breaks, and naturally he's missing a few fingers, but the worst was a log that rolled downhill and trapped him up against another log. His partner cut him out of that situation, but if he'd been alone, he could have lost both legs or worse. I told him about a logger in New Hampshire I had heard of whose arm got trapped under a tree for six hours before anyone found him. It took the doctors three times that long in the operating room to save his arm. But it would never be 100 percent again, so when he got out of the hospital, logging was no longer a career option.

He'd been a patient in the hospital for a long time—so long that it impressed him as a pretty good place to work. Never one to be waylaid by life's tribulations, he went back to school and became an OR technician, working the pump crew, charged with the task of keeping the patient's heart beating during surgery, saving lives and limbs, as his had been saved. On the weekends in the summer he goes to his Winnepesaukee lake house and sits on his porch with a brass potato cannon that he's spent considerable time and money perfecting, drinking beer and blasting big Maine russets at the yachts in the harbor. Because hey, once a Brush Cat, always a Brush Cat. Ray liked that story.

I was poking around in a storage area of Ray's shop when I stumbled upon his recycling.

"Good God, Ray," I said. "You drink your share of Diet Pepsi."

"Aww, you caught me," he said, dropping his chin to his chest. "That's right, I'm an alcoholic. Drinking and me were not meant for each other. It got so bad so one night in 1979 I started to cutting wood until I never wanted another drink. Forty-seven hours straight I cut wood—the sun came up and went down twice during that time and finally I broke the alcohol's spell over me. After that I told myself if I ever drank another drop, I'd have to cut wood even longer to quit again. So I never have, and life's been good."

I had merely commented on the volume of Diet Pepsi he consumed; I hadn't meant to get into his shit. Actually I had been thinking of giving him a lecture on the evils of aspartame, but after that I just nodded and patted him on the shoulder.

My kids had recently installed a couple of angora rabbits in the barn—my twelve-year-old daughter plans to become a bunnie tycoon someday—so I picked a beautiful carved rabbit off Ray's gallery wall for them to hang on the stall door where the rabbits lived.

"How much?" I asked.

"Forty bucks," said Ray.

I handed him two twenties and said, "My last forty bucks."

Ray rubbed the bills together and put them in his pocket. "My first forty bucks," he said, smiling.

Not too far from Ray's place over in Bar Harbor is *Timber Tina's Lumberjill Show,* which is damn near as popular as a lobster dinner with the tourists. Beautiful, sweaty women doing lumber sports on a hot August evening, the whine of the saws, the smell of the sawdust—it's just plain good family fun. Tina, who was once a contestant on *Survivor,* comes from a family of timber-sport enthusiasts and, like Ray, makes a living doing what she loves.

Not surprisingly, Timber Tina's big sister, Judy Hoeschler, is the seven-time women's logrolling champion.

"She's got five feet," said her former coach and husband, Jay Hoeschler.

Judy and Jay are too fit and good-looking to be my age, but

there you have it. Clean, active living pays off. I've tried logrolling, and while I'm reasonably sure I could manage to perform any of the other timber-sport events—not particularly well or fast enough to actually compete, of course—logrolling is something I'll never manage. It's like snowboarding—I just caught my edges and face-planted into the cold hard snow too many times to ever pick it up. It was one of the things that would kill me long before I learned it. Like logrolling. In my mind, snowboarding plus logrolling equals water boarding.

Judy was a natural from the age of twelve, when she picked it up in her hometown of Hayward, Wisconsin, then learned formally from a woman named Marlis Hodd. Marlis's job was to logroll for the customers at the Wannegan Diner, located in the heart of History Land in Hayward. History Land and the Lumberjack Bowl—a sports stadium dedicated to timber sports— were built by Tony Wise, a Hayward real estate developer who, after World War II—once the lumberjacks had cut down all the trees—started buying and selling lots to people from Chicago, Minneapolis, and St. Paul. Tony had vision and big ideas. And he loved logrolling. His primary project was a resort in Hayward, and, as a way to attract tourists, he became logrolling's biggest booster.

The first Lumberjack Bowl was held in 1960, and timber sports grew exponentially from there, due in large part to Tony Wise's canny sense of promotion. As side acts for the World Logrolling Championships, he invited the guys who competed in lumberjack competitions at county fairs. And the spectacle we know as timber sports was born. The first year there were 125 people in the five-thousand-seat arena. But within three years,

Tony had ABC's "Wide World of Sports" covering the event. Tony Wise didn't invent timber sports, but he repackaged them for mass consumption. The championships are held annually in July and the event packs them in. When I made a reservation at a motel in Hayward, I asked the desk clerk on the phone how close to the Lumberjack Bowl I'd be.

"As close as you'd want, I'd think," she said.

Marlis's job, at first anyway, was simply to logroll outside the restaurant to the amazement of the flatlanders there to experience History Land; this gathering of many of Hayward's historically significant buildings was dismantled before the demolition ball struck and reconstructed as a logging village. They sold tickets and bric-a-brac, naturally.

Marlis thought simply logrolling all day outside the Wannegan was kind of boring, so she offered lessons instead. Judy joined up that first year and won her national division three years later.

"There were three of us competing," she said.

"And she won her first world championship three months after our first child was born," said Jay. She went on to six more world championships, as well as competing in the CBS's "Superstars," and ABC's "Battle of the Sexes." *Superstars* is a multidisciplined event, none of which has anything to do with any individual-athlete's sport—obstacle courses, rock climbing, that sort of thing. *Battle of the Sexes* grew out of the Billie Jean King/Bobby Riggs match, which Billie Jean won. Judy rolled the male logrolling world champion on national TV.

"The guy beat me," she said, "but I beat him at another event the next year."

184 © BRUSH CAT

Hayward birlers dominate the logrolling world and it started after Judy's trip to *Superstars,* where she had access to new strength, agility, and endurance training. She brought her newly acquired techniques home and shared them—Hayward birlers romped the sport for years after that. Still do.

"But, you know, the effect of television and high-level training wasn't necessarily what you'd expect, because I saw a drop-off in participation then," Judy said. "People lost interest in competing because they couldn't beat the tough crew from Hayward. You can't imagine how discouraging it is to be the best birler in Connecticut or New Jersey—a fairly solitary undertaking that requires thousands of hours in the cold water—only to go to the world championships every year to get dunked in the first round by some third-stringer from the Hayward contingent."

When her daughters began competing (they've now gone on to win a slew of championships of their own), she found it hard to coach them and then compete against them.

"It was hard to roll my kids," she says wistfully. So she retired early. Some (Jay) would say too early.

Wood inspires these circuses, as anyone who watches ESPN or the Outdoor Life Network can attest. Timber sports were once nearly as omnipresent on cable TV as bobble-heads gossiping about politics and the stock market. The games remain hugely popular in the United States and the United Kingdom, but it turned out to be a tough business model for television. There are few, if any, natural advertisers, and no product placement opportunity.

You'd think that pickup trucks and fast food might be a good fit—that an audience is an audience. But marketing is an increasingly vertical science that trolls for can't-lose connections between what people are seeing and what you can make them want. Power sports are popular now because they can advertise four-wheelers, motorcycles, snowmobiles, helmets, boots, jackets, trailers, etc. But nobody's manufacturing logs, or making shoes to roll in. Joe Sixpack might watch timber sports on a Saturday afternoon, but he's not going to run out and buy a Stihl chainsaw on Sunday. What would he do with it? But a snowmobile—with that he can get drunk and drive ninety miles an hour across the lake. Not that a majority of sledders do that sort of thing; just the ones I read about in the paper.

Timber sports are exciting because the events are modeled on what loggers actually do, or at least did—scale giant trees and cut their tops off, logrolling, handsaw cutting, chainsaw cutting, ax tossing, and speed chopping. It's all very noisy and reasonably dangerous, like NASCAR for the outdoors type. And logrolling is the most exciting of the lot—it has speed, endurance, strategy, tactics, and eventually somebody falls on their arse and into the icy drink. Great entertainment.

"ESPN tried it for six years with the *Great Outdoor Games* and then pulled the plug," Jay explained. "It was a boon to the sport at first, but unfortunately there was no governing body to represent the sport or its athletes. Logrolling is basically unregulated, which made it attractive to programmers in the first place. There was no Olympic committee or other membership organization to negotiate with—it was free sailing for the legal department.

There was an international logrolling organization—which I ran for a while—but not a national chapter, and certainly no state and local outfits. And that was a problem. A sport needs to grow organically, from the grass roots, with people doing it locally, competing against other athletes from their county and state, then going to national match-ups."

"A sport needs a broad base long before it's on television," said Judy, ". . . otherwise it's entertainment rather than competition. And that, I think, is what has happened to logrolling and other timber sports."

But that's okay, because Judy and Jay continue to organize the sport—they're currently setting up sister-city relationships to create birlers around the world. Their most stubborn obstacle is that virtually every nation's import regulations exclude individual logs, and other such organics, from international transport because of bugs and mold and who knows what else. So the Hoeschlers are developing a hollow polymer log that uses water as its ballast and when broken down into three four-foot pieces can be easily and legally transported anywhere. Because if they can help it, a little thing like international law is not going to stand in the way of logrolling.

Another pair of world-class Hayward, Wisconsin birlers is Tina Salzman and her younger brother Darrell "Jr." Salzman. Between them they've won sixteen world championships.

After winning his sixth title at the 2005 games, Salzman's army reserve unit was deployed to Iraq. Four days before Christmas in 2006, Salzman updated his blog, "Lumberjack in the Desert," with this entry:

> It is hard for me to tell you all this but I was hurt by an IED here. My right arm has been amputated below the elbow, my left hand has four working fingers. My legs are fine so I can still logroll! I am on my way to the hospital in Germany, then back to the states for more care. I am in high spirits. I am going to be OK, but I will have a long road to recovery.

And he has, but remains determined.

"I'm definitely going to logroll again," says Salzman, "I still have my legs and five more world championships to win to catch up with my sister."

Rusty DeWees isn't just a logger, he's "The Logger." Twenty years ago in a play called "Judevine," he played a logger—not a theatrical stretch for him since, among other things, he's done his share of work in the woods. "Judevine" taught him a lot of things about theater—most important, that audiences love real talk about real things, cussing included.

Since 1997 he's been a one-man show in every sense of the word, just like nearly every other logger I've ever met. He created The Logger brand of live shows, merchandise (including DVDs, duct-tape thongs, calendars, corporate confabs, and endorsement deals), he runs the business he calls Rusty D. Inc., and, for good measure, writes all his own material. From a short theater piece that began as a one-off lark, he now nets a comfortable six-figure income. And he never has to pull a chainsaw.

Rusty's a Renaissance man of the venerated art form called regional humor. He'd like to go to the big show, but he's happy where he is. He should and probably will break in—he's as talented as anyone doing national stand-up, smarter than their agents, and has more stamina than their personal assistants.

Rusty is a lean six feet four, like a stick man made out of steel cable, with an angular face and light red hair. In his act he wears the requisite duct-tape-enhanced and unlaced logging boots, a stocking cap that—I'm guessing—he found on the side of the road at the end of winter one year; his work shirt is tattered and sleeveless, under which is a T-shirt you wouldn't wear to change your oil, and his jeans are so torn that they barely qualify as pants. He's an "ack-tor," but he's also his own wardrobe director.

Rusty moved to Vermont from Philadelphia forty years ago, when he was seven years old, which means he's not a "Vermonter." He makes this admission at every show so that real Vermonters won't get the idea that he's trying to pass. In other places you might not be a "native Californian" if you weren't actually born in-state, but eventually you become a Californian if only by virtue of having an address and a tan. A "born New Yorker" is different from those who arrived there later in life, but in the end Brooklyn-born Woody Allen is no more a New Yorker than Tom Wolfe, who began life as a Virginian. Only in Vermont can you spend 99 percent of your life there and still not be one of them. Not that it's automatically a bad thing—it's simply an inescapable distinction and a point of pride for those who can claim it. And there's nothing you can do about it.

Vermonters aren't strictly parochial; former Governor Howard Dean and U.S. Senator Bernie Sanders are both from New York. But nobody better catch them calling themselves Vermonters. Besides, the state's population has more than doubled since Rusty's family moved to Stowe in 1968, and most of the newcomers are from New York.

Rusty's dad was fifty years old when Rusty was born. He was a Greyhound bus driver on the Montreal to New York City route, his mom was a homemaker, and Rusty ". . . wasn't a very good student, but I was a funny kid. I liked basketball and trucks and cars, acting in plays . . . and my plan was to become a Greyhound bus driver as soon as I turned twenty-six, which was the minimum age, probably still is. My dad raised me to believe that the thing in life is to have a good job, and a good job was one where you wore a uniform and got a pension. I got out of high school with eight years to kill before I could apply to Greyhound, so I worked around."

Rusty was a 'creter, which is one who works on a crew building forms and pouring concrete for basements. "It's bone-marrow-aching work, but addictive," he says. There was a guy around my town who owned one of those operations a while back, Cement-Head Ed, and everyone said Ed's rich family bought him the company. I thought I'd put the logical lie to this when I asked, cheekylike, "If your parents were rich and they'd buy you a company, is that the business you'd choose?" Because I wouldn't. But apparently some people might.

Rusty also did some landscaping and logging, of course, drove dump trucks, and pumped gas. For a couple years it was a perfect life, because he also got to play town-team basketball. He was good at hoops—good enough for the coach at Champlain College in Burlington to offer him a full scholarship if he'd come play for him. *What the hell,* Rusty thought, *I got time to kill.*

When he finished college, he went back to pumping gas and playing town team. But the acting he'd done in high school was always on his mind—he liked it, and he wanted to do more of it. But it was like basketball: he had no thought of becoming a professional actor; it seemed about as likely as playing in the NBA.

"It's not as if I was going home at night thinking I'm going to be an actor. Even after I'd done a bit more of it, it wasn't something I was considering as a career. I just enjoyed the hell out of it."

Rusty found parts with the Vermont Repertory Theater doing plays by Sam Shepard and Chekhov, and there he began to learn the craft.

"Robert Ringer was the director of the Vermont Rep and he was doing real plays. Stuff that was eye-opening for me. The language, the situations, they taught me that the audience wants what's real—with a twist, sure—but people want what's true."

Rusty was twenty-six by then, old enough to be a Greyhound bus driver, old enough to get that real job. A couple of days before he was scheduled to take the UPS driver's test—Greyhound wasn't hiring—Robert Ringer called him about a new play called *Judevine,* by Vermont playwright David Budbill. "You'd be great for it," he said. "There's definitely a part in it for you, maybe more than one."

He took his UPS driving test and did well. At the end of the shift—seven P.M.—the supervisor who rode along with him congratulated him said he thought Rusty would make a good UPS driver someday.

Rusty, squirming inside, asked him, "If I take this job, will I be able to act in plays—will I have the time?"

"No, you won't."

"Will I be able to play town-team basketball?"

"No," he said.

"Then thank you, but I'm going to have to pass," Rusty told him. "If I've cost the company any money, I'll pay it back. But I want to be in this play *Judevine* awful bad, and I don't think I'm ready to give up on doing it quite yet."

"That's okay," the UPS man told him. "We'd rather you told us now than later."

Rusty got the part—in fact he got three parts—in *Judevine,* including the role of a logger—a role for which, without realizing it, he'd been preparing for a long time.

After touring with four different productions of *Judevine,* Rusty got the idea that being an actor might be a real job for him after all. He remembered traveling with his dad down to New York City on the Greyhound bus, and that, he decided, was where he should be. Give it a try, why not. Rusty's a game guy. With two thousand dollars and not much else, he lit out for New York City and found himself a room—the Irish landlady took pity and gave him a towel and a little radio to listen to. Having absolutely no idea how to go about being a New York actor— he'd never had an acting lesson and didn't know a soul in the business—he sat in his room for a couple of weeks listening to the Knicks on that little plastic radio, wondering what he was supposed to do next.

His mother called one day to say that she'd run into the mother of a friend of his from high school whose boy had gotten a job with the William Doyle Gallery, a Manhattan antiques dealer. She suggested that Rusty look for work there, too. So he did, and Bill Doyle hired him as his driver; before long, he was his right-hand man and confidant. For the next six years he learned how to run a successful business from a master. And it was a schooling that would not go to waste.

"I went from pumping gas on the Shelburne Road in Burlington to having lunch with Gloria Vanderbilt at 21. I signed for my suits at Barneys and Brooks Brothers, I bought a house in Vermont, and, after the first year, took the summers off to go back home, work landscaping, and play summer stock. I was happy."

Then he started getting independent-film work. Vermont writer/director Jay Craven cast him in *Where the Rivers Run North,* and a still from the movie picturing Rip Torn and Rusty ran in *The New York Times.*

"I copied that picture, sent it to a hundred agents, got ten replies."

One summer day in Vermont he helped a friend shovel gravel onto a driveway. The house belonged to Benjamin Hendrickson, a soap opera star, and Rusty's buddy told him all about how Rusty was trying to act in New York City, what a big talent he was, blah blah blah. Hendrickson had heard it all before, but Rusty was somehow different. Hendrickson liked Rusty's look, so, back in New York he introduced him to his commercials agent—which turned out to be another big boon to The Logger's career.

"My first ad was for Citroën, but my first U.S. national commercial was for Kellogg's Corn Flakes. They needed a Mainer fisherman, with the accent. It shot on San Pedro Pier in L.A. At the call-back they had a dialogue coach, and though I beat up the Maine accent, she had nothing to say, thought it was great, and I wondered why. Also, I ended up ad-libbing the spot—the director was cool.

"Then I did four spots for Wendy's, two for Chevy trucks ('Like a Rock'), Coke, Sharp, Hardee's, Renault, Bayer, Aleve, Fidelity Funds, some beer—I forget which one—and bunches more. They were great to do, and basically how I learned to act on film. I never sat in the trailer, I always watched what was going on. Get paid to learn, can't hardly beat that."

He's now done twenty-five feature films, a handful of soap operas, a couple of *Law & Orders* . . . and in 1997, at thirty-seven years old, he had a great job (no uniform or pension, but still a great job) and was acting in New York City. Which, considering that more people go to New York every year to become actors than to visit the Statue of Liberty, success on any discernible level is a minor miracle. But he never felt like a New Yorker; he regarded it more as a work posting than a home. After eleven years, he gave New York up to become The Logger.

Driving back and forth from New York to Stowe every weekend (his dad was getting older and he wanted to spend more time with him), he began writing bits about the people he worked with on cement crews and in the woods. Funny stuff.

"I thought it was funny, anyway," he said. "And I don't call it writing, I call it making stuff up. I was interested in what those guys thought, how their minds worked, the things in life that got and kept their attention, the things they ignored, all that stuff."

He'd write the bits down, practice them, and try them out on his buddies. They thought it was pretty funny, too. Another buddy of his was putting on a talent show in Waterbury, Vermont—the *Groundhog Opry*—and Rusty signed up.

"This was something different," Rusty explained. "I'd been onstage all my life, but always with other people's work. This time it was my own stuff." Rusty learned the same lesson every actor-turned-writer/director learns: as an actor you only have to worry about whether you're doing it well; as a writer, you worry if it's any good.

Vermont people are usually an unforgiving audience, and they loved it. Was it the glottally punctuated speech pattern they took to? "Frick'n" is a term central to Rusty's logger schtick. There's a way to say it right, and a way to say it like an old boss of mine. The way to say it correctly is to sound like you really want to say "fuckin'," but for whatever reason, you can't. The wrong way to say it is to sound like you think frick'n is dirty, rather than a perfectly acceptable excuse for a word that really is dirty. The way flatlanders say "frick'n" makes it sound like "goldarn it." Say what you mean, because if you use "goldarn it" or "Jezum Crow," I can assure you that God knows goddamn well what you really meant.

The Logger's native dress was impressive—far more anthropologically correct than anything you'll find in the Museum of Modern History. But his appeal, I believe, is mostly Rusty—

his broad, sweeping basso, the way he moves onstage like a slow-motion ninja, the smile, the frown, the mock disgust. The content is precisely what comedy is made of—a matter-of-factness about things generally left unsaid. Like how long his girlfriend pees in the morning or how people are "Wal-Mart smart—plenty in the store but none of it worth a shit."

One Vermont reviewer explained the revolutionary importance of the show's success, "We don't even clap for our kids in school plays around here. This was funny." That's because it was more than comedy; it was theater.

With his triumphant *Groundhog Opry* success, Rusty booked five shows at Burlington's First Night celebration. They put a cussing disclaimer on the sign out front because it's a family event. Still, people happily brought their kids with their Lake Champlain–frigid-windblown-painted faces into the hall. We took our kids to these things when they were small and it would be so cold out that we'd scan the program for shows that looked unlikely to have a line. I don't know if that's what happened to Rusty that New Year's Eve, but he filled and slayed the room five times that night.

"These were Burlington people," he said. "And up until that point I wasn't really sure if Burlington folks laughed at the same stuff Waterbury folks did. But they do. Everybody does."

It was then that Rusty got the idea to create his own show, take it on the road, be the master of his domain. He rented a few school auditoriums, had some posters printed (which he hung around town on phone poles and in shop windows himself), called all the newspapers, and got a crash course in advertising—start to finish, it was his soufflé; he made it rise.

196 ⊙ BRUSH CAT

His first show packed six hundred people into an elementary-school gymnasium, and by the time his tour wound up six venues later at the venerable Flynn Theater in Burlington, he had a Ben & Jerry's von Trapp Family–sized buzz going. He rented the Flynn for a Monday and a Tuesday night—the only dates available—and hit the street with posters.

"The Flynn holds fourteen hundred people, and they'll rent you just the stage, put a couple hundred chairs up there. I said no thanks, I want the Flynn, the whole theater. Well, they said, we can put a scrim up at the seven-hundred-seat mark. I said, No, I want the whole theater. Then they suggested I rent just the downstairs, and I said, No no no. I want the whole damn place."

Which was smart, because he had a thousand people on Monday and a thousand people on Tuesday; until then, "Judevine" held the Flynn Theater attendance record for Vermont-based theater events. The Logger was officially a Vermont phenom. Not quite Quechee Gorge or maple syrup, but in the same wood-lot. Nearly every little town in Vermont has an opera house, an old Grange hall, or an elementary school, anything with a stage in it, and it seemed it was Rusty DeWees's goal to play them all. And then start on the rest of the country.

He's been back in Vermont full-time again for a decade, living in a big house with wraparound porches overlooking the Green Mountains, a hot tub, four plasma televisions (including one in the bathroom), and an indoor outhouse with a sink fashioned out of an old galvanized sap bucket. It's a very cool place and far cry from his bare room with the little radio in Manhattan.

He still acts in movies and television, but his bread and butter is his Logger act. He's got five hours of material now, writes new stuff all the time, and the audiences never tire of it. He may not be a Vermonter per se, but he's definitely one of theirs. He frames life in a perspective they can relate to, cringe from, and "laugh until their backs get better." And then, faster than you can downshift a logging truck into a 9 percent incline, Rusty can tear you up with a hymn, a story about The Logger's precious wife, or a cussed-out parable about the naked humanity that lies beneath every exterior. Rusty says real loggers cut wood and make people warm on the outside; The Logger makes them warm on the inside.

"We take different roads, but we both get to the same house."

9

STAYIN' ALIVE

Believe me! The secret of reaping the greatest fruitfulness and enjoyment from life is to live dangerously.
Friedrich Nietzsche

What makes a logger a logger? If you ask a Brush Cat, it's the ability to do the job—not necessarily well or profitably or with a smile on your face, but being in the woods, cutting trees, and selling the wood—that makes you a logger.

If you ask an insurance company—especially a health insurance company—what a logger is, they might have a different definition. Is a logger someone who gets hurt while cutting a tree down? Does it matter that he's a cost analyst for Pizza Hut, or a cabdriver, or a high school geography teacher during the week? The insurers say only people whose primary occupation is logging are factored into the Workers' Compensation, life, and medical insurance data, and I have no reason to believe otherwise—especially considering that the fatality rates for loggers are the highest in the country. But even after an explanation from an insurance broker as to how rates are arrived at, I still have a much better working understanding of particle physics than I do of actuarial charts, residual market rates, and loss costs. What I do know—from the most recent New Hampshire Insurance Department report—is that the residual market rates for nonmechanized loggers is $45.48, and loss costs are $28.29. I think you add those numbers together to arrive at a rate per $100 payroll cost, or a $73.77 insurance premium for every $100 an employer spends in payroll. Which is down from previous years.

Now compare loggers at $73.77 to $28.30 for mechanized loggers, $14.67 for police officers, $23.89 for asbestos workers, and $52.56 for stunt flyers and parachuters (I'm not making that up). So, whatever those numbers mean, loggers are by far the highest-wire act working without a net that the insurers can conceive of—and they take their piece.

But most loggers I know have never been hurt seriously—or at least no more than anyone who does a physically challenging job. Bob Santy says, "We been awful lucky. But still, when somebody gets hurt or killed in the woods, most people are kind of shocked by it, but for us, it's just normal. It's what happens when you're running a chainsaw."

Loggers don't like to talk about their injuries any more than gamblers want to discuss their losses. It's simply not a fun topic, and no good can come of dwelling on bad luck. When they will talk about it is when they've seen something really stupid happen, especially if it happened to somebody they didn't like.

There are plenty of wrenched backs and pulled ligaments, the occasional bad cut, but, on the whole, the people I've spent time around are cautious and mindful of what they're doing, and somehow avoid the more horrific mishaps. Sure, they lose a finger here and there, and even the best can misjudge how a tree will fall, or how far back the butt end will jump up at you—and any of these things can land you in the hospital or in a pine box. But you don't hear about it much. And I truly hope that I haven't jinxed anybody by mentioning it.

I took a logger's first-aid class down at the Hubbard Brook Experimental Forest in Thornton, New Hampshire. It's a U.S. Forest Service outpost where scientists come to study the relationship between trees and hydrology—a subject you'd think has been studied into oblivion by now. But climate change is rewriting the script. As we move from a spruce-fir forest to a hickory-oak forest, the conifers will die off, to be replaced by broad-leaf trees, which use a lot more water. New game, new rules, new research opportunities.

But I digress, as I often do when the subject turns to human entrails outside the body, which was the subject of this training. There I was, with a dozen loggers and Tim Emperor, emergency medical technician docent. He's worked as an EMT and in hospital emergency rooms, but he's moved on to a new phase where he's training people in emergency medicine. He has two clients, two groups of people he teaches—loggers and U.S. soldiers in Afghanistan and Iraq.

"Because," he says, "they suffer similar wounds in locations where they're not likely to get to the hospital quickly enough to save their lives if they can't treat themselves first. For guys who work in the woods, there's nothing abstract about this information. Plus, I used to be a logger and I like them."

Tim has a slide show he uses for the training that's so grisly, frequent viewings might reprogram Hannibal Lecter into a vegetarian. Tim's got chopped faces, dangling limbs, crushed appendages—it's like an ad for We Are Guts, all in yawning, six-by-eight Technicolor. He was full of useful tidbits, too. If, for instance, a gloved hand is crushed—and the ways that could happen on a logging job are too numerous to list here—you should *never* remove the glove. The reason being that the hand's skin will likely come right off with it, and, from Tim's detailed description of his last encounter in the emergency room treating this condition, it's a job and a half to put back on.

Ironically, a hand with its skin removed is known in the emergency medical field as "a gloved hand." This was an interesting use of the term *gloved* as a transitive verb, I thought, and as Tim showed us the slide of the exposed blood-colored sinew and pulverized bone that used to be somebody's right hand, I was daydreaming about grammar.

At lunch, the convenience store down the road had a choice of roast beef sandwiches or pizza. I passed on both. Mercifully, after lunch the presentation shifted to CPR, which I thought I knew something about. Wrong again.

"The first-aid books you have are out of date," Tim said. "The old CPR protocol was fifteen chest compressions, two breaths, fifteen chest compressions, and et cetera. The new method is thirty chest compressions to one breath."

"More pumpin', less kissin'," shouted a logger named Mike, who looked like John Travolta wearing Larry the Cable Guy's clothes.

"Good way to remember it," Tim said.

"What's one breath do?" I asked.

"Nothing," said Tim. "It just gives you a break from all those chest compressions. Nobody needs you having a heart attack when you're trying to save somebody's life. And while we're on the subject, how *do* you know when you're having a heart attack?"

People shouted out: Sore arm! Shortness of breath! Cold sweat! Pain in your chest!

"Right," said Tim, "but why is all that information useless?"

"Because," I said, "I always have a sore arm, a sore chest, cold clammy skin, or shortness of breath."

"Exactly," said Tim. "We all present one or more of the symptoms most of the time. The answer is—and I know because it's happened to me—when you're having a heart attack, you'll know, because it'll feel like nothing else that's ever happened to you. You won't mistake it for gas."

"So when my logging partner tells me he thinks he's having a heart attack, should I believe him?" asked Travolta the Cable Guy.

"Of course," said Tim. "But what about when someone who is injured can't tell you what's wrong? Sometimes they're already unconscious when you find them. Let's say you're working a job and you come upon the forester lying unconscious in the woods. What's the first thing you do?"

"Grab his spray can and mark every tree on the lot?" asked Travolta.

"No," said Tim. "And forget about trying to find his pulse, because you never will. Get something shiny, a piece of metal or chrome—a mirror is best—and hold it under his nose to see if it fogs. That way you can tell if he's breathing. If you don't have anything shiny, you can start CPR, but you have to be careful. He could have choked on something, or hit his head."

It was all fairly confusing and scary, knowing that once you have this knowledge, you're expected to use it, but Tim put everyone at ease.

"I'm a big proponent of everyone knowing CPR," he said, ". . . and that you should administer it as well as you can for as long as you can; you also have to know that if your buddy is having a heart attack, your chances of saving him under those conditions—where no one else can get to him and help—is one, maybe two percent. Without a defib machine or a quick response from 911, the odds of survival aren't good. I tell you this so you don't beat yourself up about it if somebody you try to save in the woods dies."

"Will jumper cables work like a defib?" asked Travolta.

"Yeah, maybe," Tim said. "In fact, if you're near the skidder and you have jumpers, fire them up and put them to him. It can't hurt."

"Do you mean clamp them right on his nipples?" asked Travolta.

"No," said Tim. "Just hold them to his bare chest."

Stanching bleeding is a big topic with Tim. Depending upon which artery you've severed, the human body can bleed out in mere minutes. And you're unconscious well before that anyway. So, in the event of a large, sucking wound, the first order of business is to stop the bleeding. This can be accomplished by taking off your shirt, or finding a rag, and stuffing it into the wound, then applying pressure until the flow stops. Chainsaws make wounds you could stuff a prom gown into, and despite the less-than-sterile nature of most loggers' shirts or skeevy rags on the floor of the skidder, infection is not the primary problem. Bleeding to death quickly is.

But bleeding to death slowly can be worse. A logger stuck out in the woods alone with no phone reception and nobody who'll be looking for him if he isn't home by six, can lie there in the woods, too weak to move until the coyotes or any number of other carnivorous varmints find him and have a luau. Fortunately, Tim had no photos of the Three Bears munching on a downer Brush Cat. But it happens.

If the wound is dismemberment rather than a gouge, you may want to resort to a tourniquet. Again, this can be a piece of clothing, duct tape, wire, whatever you have handy. Then, once it's applied, you have an hour—tops—to get help before everything below the tourniquet will have to be amputated.

Tim is very matter-of-fact about the carnage. "Clinical" might be a more fair description, and it's a mind-set that you want in an emergency medical worker.

"I never stop and think, 'Oh, man, that's gross,' he said. "I simply see it as something damaged that needs repair and I get to work."

One of my oldest friends, Jimmy, is a radiation oncologist. When he can't eliminate a tumor with radiation, he sometimes has to cut it out of a person's body. Cancerous tumors, I gather, are nasty things. Anyway, Jim bought a new house and after a few weeks it began to smell. He eventually pinpointed the source as his fireplace chimney, got a mirror, looked up there, and found a dead squirrel trapped in the flu. So he grabbed a plastic grocery bag, reached up inside, and extracted the rotting, maggot-infested, bug-eyed corpse.

I asked him, "Wasn't that disgusting?"

"Compared to what?" he said.

It's that detachment I admire, because I tend to personalize everything—when my lawn mower breaks I call it every rotten-bastard name in the book, even though I know it's just a machine, that it doesn't want to be broken, that it doesn't want anything, and I'm the one who broke it anyway. Then I bitch at the grass for growing so fast.

It's Tim's ability to put anger, fear, and revulsion aside and perform the task at hand that saves lives. And I doubt that it's something that can be taught—not to me, anyway. When we lived in the city we had cable television and my daughter, who was three years old at the time, would beg me to put on Animal Planet to see if there was what she called "a blood show" on. There's nothing she liked more than watching a collie have its retina reattached, or a tumor removed from a manatee's kidney. She's thirteen years old now and wants to be a veterinarian. So I'm convinced that it's not a learned trait; it's bred in the bone, and she didn't get it from me.

There are scads of public and private studies with titles such as "Changes in Logging Injury Rates Associated with the Use of Feller-bunchers"; "Logger Deaths and Injuries by Region," etc. The titles are deceiving; it's all dry-as-dust reading. There are national and local organizations dedicated to safe logging, such as the National Timber Harvesting and Transportation Safety Foundation, Soren Erikson's "Game of Logging," the Northeast Woodland Training Institute, and many others. I've been trained in safe logging techniques and I learned a lot—but in the end, it's like safe rock climbing, or safe combat methods. Some things are just inherently dangerous.

In the real world, away from the watchful eyes and ears of qualified logging instructors, I witnessed perfect book-ended examples of how to and how not to log on adjoining woodlots just below my house last spring. In Woodlot One was Mike, a logger's logger. I'm not using his last name because he got shy after we spoke, and I didn't want to put him on the spot. He's a quiet and dignified guy, unlike most writers (me) who go around asking people personal questions, such as, "How the hell many stitches did that wound take?" He blushed.

He's been in the business since 1972, got severely injured in 1981 when his saw jumped and filleted his right biceps from his arm. After physical therapy and a long convalescence he's been back at it more than twenty years, with nary a mishap or complaint since. But he works safely. Rule number one: When you pull onto a logging site, no matter how crowded the landing is, never park where you'll block the entrance in any way. If somebody's hurt and needs to get out of there fast, they don't need to wait while you look for your car keys.

Rule number two: Always call your wife at lunchtime, tell her you're all right and where on the lot you plan to work that afternoon, and remind her what time you'll be home. More loggers' lives have been saved by their wives than by penicillin and stitches. If Mike's not home at six for dinner, or at three to take his son to baseball practice, the red flag goes up.

Wives are also great for giving tick checks at the end of the day—another valuable health benefit. In summertime, it's not uncommon to find a half dozen of them burrowed into the absolutely worst parts of your body, and not just anyone can help with that sort of thing.

Rule number three: don't work alone unless you have to. And for today's independent logger, rule three is often a tough one to keep.

Mike lives in Vermont with his family, who, as far as I can tell, are the center of his life. He cuts wood all day and rushes home for some activity with one of his children after school— usually sports related. Mike is as solid as an oak, soft-spoken, and smart. He was a ski racer in his younger days, and he still does it a bit, but coaching his kids is the real challenge now.

He's a safe logger—except he won't wear steel-toed boots because, he says, a chainsaw will bounce off the steel toe and come back at you. I've seen pictures of loggers' feet after a saw came in contact with a nonsteel-toed boot. One was cleaved in half, literally, the boot and the foot, right up the middle, like a cloven hoof. So, all due respect to Mike, but I'll stick with my steel toes. I wear them weed-whacking.

The guy in the woodlot next to Mike's was a living (for the moment) example of how not to cut wood. First, somebody dropped him off at the lot in the morning. So he worked alone with no vehicle to rush himself to the hospital, if the need arose, or at least to downtown where someone could help him. That alone could easily turn a survivable injury into a fatality. And there were a whole host of survivable injuries he was subject to because he wore no helmet, eye protection, Kevlar chaps, ear protection, or boots—he had on sneakers. When loggers get hurt badly, these are often the circumstances that precede the incident. And a foot or leg injury is the most debilitating for a logger because the first thing a feller is supposed to do when he finishes his cut is to get away from the tree as fast as possible.

"If you can't run, you can't cut," says Bob.

There are little things that we all do, such as getting a bit too relaxed and not gripping the steering wheel of our car as firmly as we should. When you cut with a saw, and you get too comfortable with it, there's a tendency to rest your thumb on the handle rather than hooked around it. When the saw jumps, you need a strong hold to maintain control of it, just like a skidding or careening car.

Christi comes from a logging family. When she and her husband, Peter, first started dating, she took him home for a holiday to meet the clan.

"He was a little embarrassed about it," she said, ". . . but he took me aside and asked, 'What's with all the missing fingers?' "

Christi's grandfather Bert was in the eighth grade when his father, Percy, a formidable Brush Cat by all accounts, informed him that if wished to continue eating, it was time to quit school and join him in the woods. Bert didn't want to, but Percy's threat wasn't idle. No work, no eat. So Bert showed him. He moved in with his grandparents, quit school, and went to work for a rival logging company with his brother Ronnie.

Their older brother Bobby got the same ultimatum and responded by joining the merchant marines. He was killed at the age of twenty-six in a work-related accident. So Bert saw his options as limited.

Ronnie was a tree sawyer, the guy on a big crew, where there's a division of labor between fellers, sawyers, and hookers, who limbs the trees and cuts them to length. He's the next wave behind the fellers, who actually cut the trees, and just before the hookers, who cable the hitches to be skidded out of the woods.

Ronnie built a reputation as one of the fastest and truest sawyers on the job. Sawyers get paid by the board foot, so, in addition to the deference of his peers, speed made Ronnie good money. One day, as he was about to clip his tape measure into a felled tree to mark it for cutting, a snag that got bumped as the tree fell toppled onto him, crushing him to death. He was thirty-six years old, moving deftly through the woods doing his job, then suddenly struck down by the delayed reaction of a rotten old tree. That's the nature of danger in the woods—unforeseen, unknowable, unstoppable. And it happens all the time.

Christi's grandfather started out as a lowly hooker and eventually bought the company. So he didn't lack for smarts or ability, but that doesn't mean he didn't lose any fingers, because he did. He also had a heart attack in the woods. The only job that will spark a cardiac event faster than logging is a fry cook who moonlights on the bomb squad. Christi simply comes from a logging family where nobody holds on to all their digits forever, and sometimes people go to work and never come home. That's being a logger. As I pound away on my keyboard, wearing my robe and Guinness Draft slippers, I think that the most dangerous thing I face is a paper cut—which I could get only because some logger cut the tree.

A logger can do everything right and still get hurt, or worse. Sometimes it's just bad luck, and when chainsaws, skidders, and falling trees are involved, bad luck tends to be very, very bad.

David Pickman, sixty years old, wiry, rolls his own cigarettes, owns a garage full of motorcycles, is an ex-logger who once flipped a skidder on a switchback and leaped from the door just as it was going over the embankment.

"Timberjacks are orange," he said ". . . and all I could see was black tires and the gray of metal undercarriage coming at me. It was like a rampaging elephant about to stomp me. But I scooted out of the way in the last moment and all it did was sort of crush my hand and rebreak my leg."

"Rebreak your leg?"

"Yeah, a couple months before, the butt end of a log came crashing into the cab and hit my right leg. Turns out it broke my tibia. I just thought it was sore, but the emergency room doctor told me it was knitting when I broke it again. Skidders are dangerous; my friend Freddie Stoukivoff was rigging a load with his skidder and he just looked back to see how it was doing when the bear-claw chain on his tire picked up a branch, spun it around, caught him in the face, and gouged out his right eye. But he was all right with it. He was back pitching for the softball team a month later. And that's hard without any depth perception."

Bob and I sat on a pile of firewood logs at his landing one morning; it was a nice day, we were talking and laughing. Then he said, "My first job cutting in the North Country was finishing up a firewood pile that a man died on. Bob Simpson. He had a reputation as a good cutter—an experienced logger known for finessing the saw. He was cutting firewood, oak and maple just like this pile, and his saw jumped up and hit him in the jugular. Happened in the fraction of a second. He just bled to death right there on the woodpile."

The smile on his face was gone.

"I'd just moved up here," he said. "I was looking for a house to buy, and I looked at his place. It was out in Landaff, nice, affordable. But then I thought, Should I be living in a dead logger's house?"

That would tempt the fates, and just being out there doing the job as safely and wisely as possible is already tempting them as much as they'll stand for—so no, if you're a logger, you don't buy a dead logger's house. Or his saw. You might make an offer on his skidder, though, if it's in good shape and he didn't die on it.

10

WORLD OF WOOD

*Geography is just physics slowed down
with trees stuck in it.*
       Terry Pratchett

Depending upon the job, loggers are at best
short-term sharecroppers and at worst migrant farm
labor. They are often maligned as wood cheats and
tree rapists, beer swillers, and street fighters. Here and there, that
all might be true. Usually not, though. In my experience, independent loggers are the swashbucklers of the woods, the giant-
killers of the Great Northern Forest, and the final ragtag American
army battling unavoidable globalization.

Both micro- and macroeconomically, the independent logger is going the way of the woolly mammoth. The North American Free Trade Agreement, and now the Central American Free
Trade Agreement, will continue to reduce the average logger's
income. They're hit from the north, outbid by Canadians with

universal heath care, and from the south by Mexicans and Central Americans with willy-nilly government regulation and logging companies with free rein to cut wherever they like. Of the seven Central American nations only Costa Rica has a highly developed system of public lands, and a culture of conservation.

In the late 1980s I lived in a Honduran village in the Department of Yoro, a remote place in an even more remote part of the country. My house had no electricity and no running water, but neither did my house in New Hampshire.

It was a magically real place—at a time when I still read that stuff—where illiterate peasants conveyed more wisdom than a roomful of rabbis, little children were mindful and compassionate, and twenty-five miles away in the city of Yoro, it actually rains fish every year. One rainy day the paupusas came—little bluish bugs that swarm like locusts for four hours and then die by the millions. It took another four hours to sweep them all up.

The village, El Rosario, was five miles up the most broken and useless dirt road I'd ever been on. It was a ladder of continuous switchbacks into and over the mountains, all the way to the Caribbean coast. A good four-wheel-drive truck could make it, but not as a regular trip. Too many times up this road and a new rig would be junk long before it was paid for.

The lack of a serviceable road was a hardship for the farmers—virtually everyone in El Rosario—the coffee growers, especially because the coffee-company trucks couldn't come to them. So they had to go to the trucks.

Fifty-pound coffee-bean bags on our backs, down, down, down the busted road, over gullies, around sink holes to the main highway, hot and sweaty, my heart pounding in my ears. This wasn't a fifty-pound rucksack designed to distribute its weight evenly for ease of carry; this was a burlap bag stuffed with coffee beans. We carried them on our heads; then I carried mine on my back, then back to my head, then like a sack of groceries, then back onto my back . . .

As I struggled next to my landlord, Mauricio, twenty years older than I and 60 percent of my size, I asked him what in hell had happened to the road, because I'd been here several years before and there had been a perfectly good road. I hadn't imagined it. It was a hard-packed dirt road, nicely graded, with well-placed water bars and convenient turnouts.

"The government built the road," he said. "Which was very good. But then the logging trucks came and destroyed the road, taking the giant pines off the mountains."

"Then why don't you ask the government to fix the road for you?"

"Because the trucks will come back," he said.

It's not just Central America, it's Eastern Europe and Indonesia, the Philippines, Africa. In Littleton, New Hampshire, seven miles from my house, I can buy twelve-inch-wide by twelve-foot-long clear yellow pine boards. The loggers call them pumpkin pine, because they're so big. And they're "clear"—no knots, which are created by branches on the trunk. This means they came from very large trees. The boards come from Siberia and they're cheaper than technically inferior boards cut and milled right here in New Hampshire. How, I ask myself—considering the shipping charges associated with the mass and weight of lumber—is that possible?

As the Russian journalist Dmitry Butrin puts it, "The forest business in Russia is like the taiga: there are no laws there, and the treetops create excellent conditions for a shadow business." The taiga is the planet's largest land-based biome, a coniferous forest that spreads from Kazakhstan to northern Japan, Alaska, Canada, Norway, Sweden, Finland, Siberia, Minnesota, New York, New Hampshire, and ends in Maine.

Russian logging and environmental regulations are every bit as stringent and incorruptible as their banking and election laws (although, let's be honest, ours are nothing to brag about either), which have resulted in old-growth Siberian forests being clear cut, milled, and shipped abroad.

The devalued ruble keeps the price down, as does the fact that the Russian logging industry is dominated by the corporate tsars who run the domestic oil industry. Unfettered access to the world's largest timber reserves, cheap labor to cut and mill it, and cheaper oil to ship it around the world add up to a market advantage that's tough to beat.

If not for its aged and deteriorating production capabilities, Russia would be a much larger player on the international forest-products scene. Capital investments in harvesters and mills could change the equation dramatically, but anyone who has driven a Russian Lada, or seen the containment vessels over their nuclear plants with less structural integrity than a well-built sukkah, knows that the Russians are not likely to manufacture high-producing feller-bunchers, skidders, forwarders, or sawmills anytime soon. But better equipment can be secured from abroad, and when it is, the U.S. forest industry will have a major new competitor.

Illegal logging in Russia, Southeast Asia—especially Indonesia and the Philippines—Latin America, and Africa costs the U.S. forest products sector $1.1 billion annually in lost sales—that's 5 percent of the industry overall, but just a small portion of the $23 billion in illegally harvested timber around the world. Despite strict laws against it here and abroad, the market for gangster wood thrives.

It's not the most likely scenario, but America faces a future when logging is no longer a way of life here, when a home-grown Brush Cat's livelihood is lost. Given the size of our forests and our appetite for wood, there'll always be a nice buck to be made in the forest-products industry, but with sinking wages and rising costs, who will do the actual wood harvesting?

Losing our logging savvy would be like the Japanese abandoning their rice-growing tradition, yet it may very well come to pass. When it's no longer financially feasible for Americans to log America's forests, others will do it for us through foreign-guest-worker programs and imports. And at some point, for practical purposes, we'll forget how. It's not a guaranteed future, but as imports become more fluid and immigration policies encourage foreign workers to fill skilled positions, it's certainly possible. It may sound as strange as the Swiss quitting clocks, or the French giving up toast, but when financial decisions about domestic industries are made solely in the context of global competition, then change is guaranteed, and fundamental change is likely. Think outsourcing, sweat shops, and lead-painted toys.

Thirty percent of the land in this country is forested—much of it wild—and the number of people who can manage and harvest it properly drops every year, replaced by highly mechanized timber operations. A Brush Cat may be an independent operator, but in the end, he works for the mill. More mills, more competition, better stumpage paid to the logger. A generation ago there were forty mills close to where I live. Today there are four. The number of loggers in New Hampshire is down to around a thousand—half of what it was twenty years ago and perhaps 5 percent of what it was less than a century ago. Not a promising trend.

11

I'M A LUMBERJACK
AND I'M NOT OKAY

The Future of Independent Logging

*The credit belongs to the man who is
actually in the arena, whose face is
marred by dust and sweat and blood, who
strives valiantly; who errs, who comes
short again and again; because there is
no effort without error and
shortcoming . . .*
Theodore Roosevelt

In 1653 the historian Edward Johnson
marveled that in one short generation, British
colonists had transformed a "remote, rocky, barren,

bushy, wild-woody wilderness," into a "second England for fertileness." This was the birth of logging in the New World, the beginning of the wood economy.

· Four hundred years ago, Europe was crowded and running out of trees, so the British lumber interests stripped the New England landscape of its tall, straight pines for use as masts on sailing ships. Later, when the East was won, the trek west was known as the "conquest of the forest."

The lumber barons—also known as "timber pirates" and "pine pigs"—ruled the wood economy from coast to coast and sea to sea. Nobody went anywhere without using wood. The railroads didn't move without wooden ties for the track, wooden cars to roll on them, or the giant timbers needed to build trestles across rivers and gorges. Nothing moved west without the railroads, and the railroads went nowhere without wood. Nor did ships, boats, buggies, sleighs, or the early automobile. Without trees and loggers, the West may not have been won.

Few of the Brush Cats of the Great Northern Forest went west. Some did, and they came back bragging on the trees out there. But it tempted very few. They stayed behind to work the mills and the woods, as they do today. In Lancaster, New Hampshire, the Garland Mill, run by the Southworth brothers and their sons, is still in operation. It sits on the bank of a small stream and is powered by a twenty-foot waterwheel to produce high-grade lumber, just as it was done in 1856, when it was built. In the morning, when they throw the switch to start the day, the clutch engages the gears and fires up all the motors at once. At that moment, the big post-and-beam building shudders from top to bottom, its floors vibrate, and its walls shiver for fifteen seconds that feel like fifteen minutes. When it ends, and the sawdust on the floor stops dancing, it brings out a small but appreciative cheer from everyone, as if to say, "Let's get to it!"

Over the past few decades, many independently owned mills have been bought by the big wood-product companies. This one, and many others, survives as a family venture, an act of love and perseverance accomplished at a small profit. In the southern part of the state there's a modern wood mill run by the Merrimack River. Not far from there, in Wilton, a fourth-generation water-powered mill turns out exquisite handmade boxes that few people in town can afford to buy.

Up until the last few decades, the lumber business retained many of its original, colonial traits. In a typical sawmill town, industrial feudalism thrived. Typically, local politicians were wholly owned subsidiaries of the mill, and the community revolved around the company because it relied upon it for everything—the workers lived in company houses, shopped at the company store, their kids attended the company school, and sick people went to the company doctor. The company controlled the local bank, the insurance agency, half the lawyers, and all the police. The typical sawmill worker lived a life of institutionalized poverty, which often ended in a violent death. So they earned their independent natures.

Things have changed, but not entirely for the better. Logging will always be inexact, badly regulated, and fatally dangerous. But since the early days of logging, the mills and the landowners have had resources, while loggers were little more than share-croppers working alone in the woods with a horse. It's always been the lonesome individual against the faceless machinations of capital and power. Now the game has been stepped up to where many of the mills are mere branches on the trunks of transnational corporations with absent owners, anonymous presidents, ephemeral boards of directors, and large, aggressive herds of lawyers, all backed up by the politicians who live in their deep, deep pockets. So it's not exactly a fair fight—but a fight it is, nonetheless, and the Brush Cat wages it daily.

In rural areas where unemployment typically runs at least 10 percent, and where they never truly recover from the last recession, working in the woods is a reasonable alternative to fast food management, the army, or leaving forever. This creates a labor climate that heavily favors the mills, and leaves loggers little room for growth, capital retention, equipment maintenance, bad weather, worse luck, or the price of fuel.

For the last two decades, new home construction has boomed in the Northeast. Condos and pressboard minimansions have grown like mold in an old-growth forest. Theoretically, when demand is increased beyond capacity, as happened with lumber after Florida's four hurricanes in 2004, the flooding of New Orleans in 2005, or when the government is preparing for war, then lumber prices rise. As do lumber profits. The logger, however, seldom sees a corresponding increment in the price he's paid by the mill. And when he does get an increase in board-foot price, it's a bump, not a windfall.

- The mortgage-market crash in 2008 hit loggers like Prohibition hit brewers. Suddenly, nobody's buying houses, nobody's building them, either, and nobody needs lumber or veneer. Until very recently, there was a glut of wood on the market to the point where it was like trying to peddle dust. As I write this, the local mills are selling finished pine boards—dried, cut, and planed—for 20 percent less than they paid for the logs. So, tit for tat, the price of logs drops by 30 percent, and more loggers drop out of the game.

Bob switched mills because he felt the wood scaler at his old mill "was fucking me a thousand feet on the scales."

At the mill, the scaler measures every log's smaller end, then measures its length, and that theoretically tells them how many board feet there are in a tree. And that's what they pay. They prescribe how big the heart of the tree may be, and penalize you if it's off-center. In that case, they cut the board in cants—strange angles that maximize the amount of veneer they can shave from the sapwood. None of this is designed to benefit the logger.

"I shipped them three loads when I first got on this lot," Bob said, ". . . but the other seven went somewhere else. I know when I go over to get my check this afternoon he's going to ask me where the rest of the wood went, but too bad. I'm loyal to them, they're a good little mill, but I ain't running a charity. The trucker wants more money, I'm getting a thousand feet less on the load, I can't afford blind loyalty. Three hundred versus three-seventeen for an average, a thousand feet of pine, that's three hundred bucks' a load difference. I can't give it away."

This storm of unfortunate circumstances is no surprise. I saw it in the price of wood shavings over the past eighteen months as the price rose by half because the mills have been cutting fewer boards and producing less chaff. Supply and demand in the forest-products industry drills all the way down to our horse's stall.

The dynamic has shifted from too much wood to too few logs. The mills are struggling with fewer deliveries because so many loggers have left the business or the logging season has passed. It's a push-me-pull-you industry, tough to maintain a happy equilibrium in, almost impossible for a small-timer— sawyers and loggers—to make a reliable living. And either way you cut it, there's a dearth of wood shavings for the horse.

In addition to the pain inflicted by the housing slump, over the last twenty-five years, hardwood pulp stumpage—that is, the price—has halved; two pulp mills that consumed 1.3 million tons a year of those chips every year have closed; climate change has made for warmer winters, longer mud seasons, and an ever-dwindling work window for loggers in the woods. The future is at best uncertain. Is this any way to run a multibillion-dollar wood economy? Is this any way to manage our most abundant natural resource? Clearly not, but it's not likely to change. I simply ask that we endeavor to appreciate loggers more fully—the essentialness of their work, the difficulties and dangers they face to ensure that the paper at the office-supply store is plentiful and cheap, that toilet paper and baseball bats and the very roofs over our heads are there for us, that electricity is generated.

There's no monument to dead loggers, no honor roll in-scribed on a plaque somewhere, no outpouring of grief outside the immediate community when some poor Brush Cat checks out in the woods. I say there ought to be. But the loggers don't care; they don't need the validation, they just need healthy woodlots, and six months a year to cut in them. And those days may simply be gone forever.

BIBLIOGRAPHY

Constantine, Albert J., Jr. *Know Your Woods: A Complete Guide to Trees, Woods, and Veneers*. Revised by Harry J. Hobbs. Guilford, Conn.: Lyons Press, 2005.

Dobbs, David, and Richard Ober. *The Northern Forest*. White River Junction, Vt.: Chelsea Green Publishing, 1996.

Edlin, Herbert L. *What Wood Is That? A Manual of Wood Identification*. New York: Viking Press, 1969.

Frost, Robert. *The Notebooks of Robert Frost*. Edited by Robert Faggen. Cambridge, Mass.: Harvard University Press, 2006.

Heinrich, Bernd. *The Trees in My Forest*. New York: HarperCollins, 1997.

Klyza, Christopher McGrory, and Stephen C. Trombulak, *The Future of the Northern Forest*. Middlebury, Vt: Middlebury College Press, 1994.

Kricher, John. *A Field Guide to Eastern Forests, North America*. Illustrated by Gordon Morrison. Boston: Houghton Mifflin, 1988.

Labbe, John T., and Lynwood Carranco. *A Logger's Lexicon: An Illustrated Reference for Logging Terms and Technology*. Hillsboro, Ore.: Timber Times, 2001.

Lansky, Mitch. *Beyond the Beauty Strip: Saving What's Left of Our Forests*. Camden East, Ontario: Old Bridge Press, 1993.

Marchand, Peter J. *North Woods: An Inside Look at the Nature of Forests in the Northeast*. Boston: Appalachian Mountain Club Books, 1987.

Petrides, George A. *A Field Guide to Eastern Trees: Eastern United States and Canada*. Illustrated by Janet Wehr. Boston: Houghton Mifflin, 1988.

University of New Hampshire Cooperative Extension. *Protecting New Hampshire's Water Quality*. University of New Hampshire Cooperative Extension, 2005.

Walker, Aidan, ed. *The Encyclopedia of Wood: A Tree-by-Tree Guide to the World's Most Versatile Resource*. New York: Facts On File, 1989.

Wessels, Tom. *Reading the Forested Landscape: A Natural History of New England*. Illustrated by Brian D. Cohen. Woodstock, Vt.: Countryman Press, 1997.